"Traditional" Theology & the SBC

An Interaction with, and Response to, the Traditionalist Statement of God's Plan of Salvation

"Traditional" Theology & the SBC

An Interaction with, and response to, the Traditionalist Statement of God's Plan of Salvation

---

Revised Edition

Thomas K. Ascol

Founders Press
Cape Coral, Florida

Published by
Founders Press

P.O. Box 150931 • Cape Coral, FL 33915
Phone (239) 772–1400 • Fax: (239) 772–1140
Electronic Mail: founders@founders.org
Website: http://www.founders.org

Digital Edition: ©2012 Founders Press
ePUB ISBN: 978–0–9849498–1–6
Mobi ISBN: 978–0–9849498–2–3

Revised Edition for Print: ©2018 Founders Press

Printed in the United States of America

ISBN 13: 978–1–943539–11–6

Contents

Preface to the Revised Edition 7

Introduction 11

1. Interacting with the Preamble 14

2. The Preamble (Part 1) 17

3. The Preamble (Part 2) 20

4. Interacting with Article One:
The Gospel 28

5. Interacting with Article Two:
The Sinfulness of Man 32

6. Interacting with Article Three:
The Atonement of Christ 41

7. Interacting with Article Four:
The Grace of God 48

8. Interacting with Article Five:
The Regeneration of the Sinner 52

9. Interacting with Article Six:
The Election to Salvation 58

10. Interacting with Article Seven:
The Sovereignty of God 64

11. Interacting with Article Eight:
The Free Will of Man 69

12. Interacting with Article Nine:
The Security of the Believer 79

13. Interacting with Article Ten:
The Great Commission 84

Conclusion 86

Afterword by Dr. Tom Nettles 88

Appendix One:

"A Statement of the Traditional Southern Baptist Understanding of God's Plan of Salvation" by Eric Hankins 93

Appendix Two:

"Polemic Theology: How to Deal with Those Who Differ From Us" by Roger Nicole 102

Preface to the Revised Edition

Six years ago, in 2012, the "Statement of Traditional Southern Baptist Understanding of God's Plan of Salvation" was published by a a group of concerned church and denominational leaders in order to assert their doctrinal convictions vis-à-vis the resurgence of the doctrines of grace (which also go by the nickname of "Calvinism") within the Southern Baptist Convention (SBC). Eric Hankins, who was at the time the pastor of the First Baptist Church of Oxford, Mississippi (and currently serving the First Baptist Church of Fairhope, Alabama in the same position) is the primary author of the document. The energy behind this efforts seems to have coalesced into a movement to promote this understanding of salvation throughout the SBC.

"Connect 316" (with the numbers presumably based on John 3:16) is the name of the organization that promotes this movement. Rick Patrick, pastor of the First Baptist Church of Sylacauga, Alabama was its Founding Executive Director. In an article posted on the Theological Matters website sponsored by Southwestern Baptist Theological Seminary, Connect 316 is described as a "ministry fellowship embracing the Traditional stream of salvation doctrine in Southern Baptist life as opposed to the Calvinist stream." They sponsor events and host the SBCToday blog.

Despite my disagreement with many of the theological positions expressed in the TS, I am very grateful that those who have published and signed the statement have been willing to declare their faith in writing. That is a good and properly Baptist thing to do and it allows for the kind of critique and dialog that I offer here.

Though I try to make it clear at various points in what follows, it should be clearly noted that, though I have serious concerns with what the TS asserts, I have genuine respect for many who have signed it. In addition, I agree with them on vital biblical truths—such as the Trinity of God, the fully deity and humanity of Christ and the inerrancy of Scripture. These are no small areas of agreement and should not be taken for granted or lost in the midst of fraternal debate.

Tom Ascol, 2018
Cape Coral, Florida

For I am God, and there is none else; I am God, and there is none like Me,

Declaring the end from the beginning, and from ancient times the things that are not yet done, saying, My counsel shall stand, and I will do all My pleasure:

Calling unto the ravenous bird from the east, the man that executeth My counsel from a far country: yea, I have spoken it, I will bring it to pass; I have purposed it, I will also do it.

—Isaiah 46:9–11, KJV

"That's our God! Now that's what you call foreordination. That's what you call predestination! That's Calvinism! And I am a Calvinist. That's good old Bible doctrine, and I believe the Bible! These things are in God's hands, and ultimately and finally, He purposed it and executeth all of it!"

—W.A. Criswell

Introduction

On May 30, 2012 I had a document emailed to me that was sent out to what looked to be a list of all the executive directors of state conventions in the Southern Baptist Convention. The title of the document is "A Statement of Traditional Southern Baptist Understanding of God's Plan of Salvation" (TS). One of the pastors who sent it to me prevailed on me to review and respond to the document.

After reading the document carefully, I quickly came to two conclusions. First, I realized that it is a serious doctrinal statement and therefore worthy of serious evaluation. I determined to give time to studying its affirmations and denials in light of the authors' claims of being both biblical and representative of the "traditional" Southern Baptist view of salvation. The second conclusion I reached is that this TS, more than anything else that I have seen written on the differences that characterize many Southern Baptists on the doctrines of grace, has the potential seriously to disrupt the fragile unity that exists in the SBC. The Great Commission Resurgence (GCR) that has been led by Southern Baptist statesmen like Johnny Hunt, Danny Akin and Thom Rainer has encouraged SBC churches to unite and rally around our common commitment to make Jesus Christ known throughout the world. Though at times tentative, and not being without its dissidents and detractors, the GCR has helped foster genuine cooperation around the gospel. My fear is that the TS will be used to revive old suspicions and misrepresentations that too often have characterized past debates over the doctrines of grace.

The list of original signers included Jerry Vines, Jimmy Draper, Paige Patterson, Malcolm Yarnell, David Allen, Eric Hankins, Emir Caner, Adam Harwood and David Hankins—men highly esteemed by Southern Baptists as pastors, SBC presidents, seminary and college administrators and professors. Within a few months of its publication, the TS garnered over six hundred signatures, including the presidents of two of the six Southern Baptist seminaries (along with several of their faculty members). Though this number represents only .0000375 percent of all Southern Baptists, it is nevertheless significant because of the prominence and influence of many of the signers.

I have no interest in participating in any unnecessary quarrels with my fellow Southern Baptists. Neither do I care about denominational politics. But I do care about truth and especially the purity of the gospel. It is out of this latter concern, and with deep respect for many of the signers of the document that I have responded. Many of the issues that they raise are of vital importance. It is time for Southern Baptists to address them plainly and thoughtfully. It is my hope that the chapters in this booklet (which originally appeared as blog posts on the Founders website, founders.org) will help serve that purpose.

Please join me in praying that the inevitable theological conversation resulting from the TS will not degenerate into personal attacks or be carried out in a way that dishonors our Lord. Rather, may He grant us humility born of submission to His Word that will enable all who engage to speak the truth in love. And may He in that process be pleased to grant us genuine spiritual and theological renewal that will empower us to preach the gospel and live out of the power of its resources with such joy and zeal that we cannot help but spend and be spent to make Christ known to the nations.

1

Interacting with the Preamble

SBC Today has posted the text of "A Statement of Traditional Southern Baptist Understanding of God's Plan of Salvation" on their site.[1] In the chapters that follow, I want to interact with the document in hopes of fulfilling the spirit of our late brother, Roger Nicole's, admonitions on "How to Deal with Those Who Differ with Us."[2]

Though I am not ashamed to be known as a Calvinist by those who have an accurate historical and theological understanding of the term, it is not a badge I intentionally wear. Having held my theological convictions on this issue for over 30 years, I don't know how anyone could honestly call me a "new" Calvinist. I do have many young friends who could perhaps accurately be put into that camp, however. It grieves me to see

[1] http://sbctoday.wpengine.com/an-introduction-to-"a-statement-of-the-traditional-southern-baptist-understanding-of-god's-plan-of-salvation"/ [accessed April 6, 2018]. See also Appendix 1.

[2] See Appendix 2.

them maligned and the doctrinal convictions which we share in common—and which we have repeatedly, publicly, historically and confessionally tried to articulate—misrepresented. Contrary to what the framers of the TS assert, I hope (and suspect) that their judgments and views are far less representative of Southern Baptists than what they boldly assert.

At the outset I want to state plainly that, though I disagree not only with many of the theological expressions of this document but also with what I see as several implied and stated misrepresentations, I am grateful for the clarity with which the authors have stated their views. For the most part, there is no difficulty understanding what they are affirming and denying. That is always helpful in theological dialogue. Furthermore, none of my critiques should be interpreted as suggesting that I think the originators of this document have no right to issue it or to argue strenuously—dare I say, aggressively—for their views. Surely Christian pastors, scholars and theologians should be mature enough to handle pointed, ruthlessly biblical debate. That does not mean "mean-spirited." It means doggedly determined to follow Scripture and to press each other to do so without apology.

I believe the Traditionalist Statement to be unwise. As I have stated previously, I think it has more potential to provoke serious division than anything else I have read on this issue coming from within the Southern Baptist camp. Given some of the debates and shenanigans that have gone on in the attacks and counter-attacks on Calvinism over the last twenty years, that is a bold statement. However, I believe that the potential divisiveness might, by the grace of God, be negated and that the ensuing result could help clarify the attitudes and convictions of several key Southern Baptist leaders. Words have meaning and are a reflection, Jesus said, of what's in the heart. There is a spectrum of views on Calvinism within the SBC. At one extreme we have Calvinists who would be happy to run all non-Calvinists out of the convention (or at least relegate them to the arena of "being tolerated"). Their counterparts on the other extreme—the anti-Calvinists—have the same agenda but with their guns aimed, obviously, at the Calvinists.

This document helps position its framers and signatories on this spectrum for all to see. That will ultimately prove to be helpful as Southern Baptists come to terms with the increasingly inescapable decision of how we will live together in the SBC. Will we demand complete uniformity on each of the doctrines clustered around salvation? Will we merely tolerate those who disagree with us at any point? Or will we choose to walk together in unity with all who agree with the Baptist Faith and Message without crossing their fingers?

2

THE PREAMBLE (PART 1)

The preamble to this document identifies the precipitating issue that called it forth as "the rise of a movement called 'New Calvinism' among Southern Baptists."[3] Though *TIME* Magazine popularized "New Calvinism" (NC) as one of the "10 Ideas Changing the World Right Now"[4] in 2009, the framers of this statement infuse the term with their own prejudices by describing it as being characterized by "an aggressive insistence on the 'Doctrines of Grace' ('TULIP')." Of course, one man's aggression is simply another man's passion, but the authors have been called to action by their perception that the NC movement is committed to two goals: 1) "advancing in the churches an exclusively Calvinistic understanding of salvation" and to 2) "making Calvinism the central Southern Baptist position on God's plan of salvation."

[3] The text to the Preamble is included in Appendix 1.

[4]http://content.time.com/time/specials/packages/article/0,28804,1884779_1884782_1884760,00.html [accessed April 6, 2018].

The first of these charges raises a question as to the signatories' attitude toward the autonomy of local Southern Baptist churches. If a church prayerfully and carefully calls a man to serve its membership as pastor, should those members not expect that pastor to "advance" his understanding of what the Bible teaches about salvation and to do so "exclusively?" I, for one, could hardly respect a man who did anything less, regardless of his theological convictions. If a Baptist church calls an Arminian to be its pastor, then do we have any right to be alarmed if that man "advances an exclusively [Arminian] understanding of salvation?" Wouldn't the same be true if the church called a Molinist or Dispensationalist? We may lament and regret such a move, but should we be alarmed at a pastor and church for acting under the authority of Christ in advancing their understanding of Bible doctrine "exclusively?"

On the second charge, perhaps Hankins, Patterson, Vines, et al. are privy to documents that spell out this agenda. If so, it would be enlightening to know exactly how the NC movement plans to proceed and furthermore, how will they know when they have achieved making their views the "central Southern Baptist position?" Once again, if the concern is that Calvinists want everyone to believe what they believe, then what alternative would the framers of this document propose for truth loving pastors of any theological stripe? Surely they would not advocate that anyone—Calvinist or not—hold their views on salvation with a *"que sera, sera"* attitude.

I do not know any Calvinist who has an agenda to make Calvinism "the central Southern Baptist understanding of salvation." It certainly is not my agenda. Although I would love for everyone to read Scripture the way that I do, I am content to live within the SBC under the doctrinal umbrella of the Baptist

Faith and Message 2000 and to cooperate with my less-Calvinistic brothers and sisters who are willing to do the same.

It seems that behind this second charge there must be some underlying concern that perhaps is not fully articulated in the preamble. I am speculating here and am willing to be corrected, but if the concern is that Calvinists are acting sinfully or unethically in trying to promote their views then let that be clearly stated. If there is a plot or conspiracy to make Calvinism "the central Southern Baptist position," then the authors would help us by making that known. Otherwise, their assertion of such is gratuitous and reveals that they are warring against a straw man of their own creation.

3

The Preamble (Part 2)

Though I am tempted to work through the Preamble statement by statement, I do not want to get bogged down in this part of the document to the neglect or deemphasis of its theological affirmations and denials. Neither do I want to miss the forest for the trees and thereby fail to understand the stated concerns that spawned the document. So, I will first try to summarize the overall rationale for the document and then try to offer some constructive critiques of the Preamble.

Summary of the Rationale

In essence, I believe that those who have published it are concerned by the rise of Calvinism among Southern Baptists at all levels of convention life, from local churches all the way down to various institutions and agencies. They think that Calvinism represents the views of only a small minority while their own views represent the vast majority of Southern Baptists. They are concerned to be identified positively by what they do believe rather than negatively by what they do not believe ("non-Calvinist"). They have offered this document as a testimony to their beliefs and invite other Southern Baptists to sign it to show just how many agree with their views. By doing so, they do not want to intimidate or exclude Southern Baptist Calvinists, but rather are interested in asserting what they are convinced that most Southern Baptists believe on the doctrine of salvation.

Critique of the Rationale

In no particular order I will list several points that I find problematic with the rationale for the document as stated in the Preamble.

1. **The authors authoritatively set themselves up as spokesmen for the "majority" of Southern Baptists,** stating 1) "the majority of Southern Baptists do not embrace Calvinism," 2) "the Southern Baptist majority has fellowshipped happily with its Calvinist brethren while kindly resisting Calvinism itself" and 3) "asserting that the vast majority of Southern Baptists are not Calvinists and that they do not want Calvinism to become the standard view in Southern Baptist life."

   My short response to this is, "Prove it," the impossibility of which highlights a problem that I could wish these brethren were as concerned about as they are Calvinism. No one—not even the FBI—can even *find* the "majority" of Southern Baptists, much less authoritatively declare what they believe. More substantively, however, is the danger of trying to do theology by majority—something that sends an icy chill up my Baptist spine. Further, when well over 60% of Southern Baptists don't even show up for worship on Sunday, I'm not sure that I would take much pride in declaring that my views represent "the majority." Finally, I can more readily prove that the "majority" of Southern Baptists deny regenerate church membership, corrective church discipline, the necessity of holiness and the authority of Scripture than the authors of this document can prove that their views of salvation represent that same majority. All I have to do is appeal to the inerrant words of our Savior, who said, "By their fruits you shall know them" (Matthew 7:15–20; cf. 21–23). The framers of this document will have to find the majority of Southern Baptists before they can ever hope to speak for them. Confidently asserting they can do so is disingenuous at best.

2. **The document makes confusing statements about Southern Baptist Calvinists.** Earlier, I dealt with the accusations regarding the supposed goals of Southern Baptist Calvinists, but it also bears noting that the Preamble makes further distinctions among this group. After making the charge that the "New Calvinism" is marked by "an aggressive insistence on the Doctrines of Grace" the statement later says that "most Southern Baptist Calvinists have not demanded the adoption of their view as the standard." So, has this document arisen out of concern for what the authors' admit to be a minority of a vast minority? If it is only a troublesome minority of Southern Baptist Calvinists who are in view, I think the framers of this document would have been well-served to include some representatives from among the majority of Southern Baptist Calvinists to help them address their concerns.

3. **The document demonstrates historical myopia in its use of the label "traditional."** Much like the desire to have

the majority behind you, I can understand wanting to claim that yours is the "traditional" view on a subject. But doing so begs the question, "whose tradition?" This was one of the tactics that liberals used during the inerrancy controversy in their attempt to discredit the conservative resurgence during the 1980s. It is sad to see those who produced this document resort to the same strategy. The Preamble goes all the way back to 1925 to establish its framers' historical credentials. The problem is that the SBC began in 1845. The document does admit that "Calvinists have been present in Southern Baptist life from its earliest days" and "some earlier Baptist confessions were shaped by Calvinism." Nevertheless, the TS claims to identify the Baptist Faith and Message of 1925 (BF&M 1925) as the benchmark for determining what is "traditional" Southern Baptist theology. Any careful reading of that document, however, reveals that it cannot, by any honest measure, be claimed to support the TS. Article III of the BF&M 1925 alone makes this abundantly clear.[5]

In his book, *By His Grace and For His Glory*, Tom Nettles has persuasively argued that Calvinism was the theological consensus for the first 70 years of the SBC. The convention's first official confession of faith, which was written to provide doctrinal boundaries for our first seminary, reflects this consensus. So, if we are going to take the complete history of the SBC into consideration, rather than an abridged version, this document would more accurately be called "A Statement of ***Modern*** Southern Baptist Understanding of God's Plan of Salvation." The understanding of salvation that was prevalent throughout the convention

[5] See Chapter 5.

at its inception and for many decades afterward was nothing less than historic, evangelical Calvinism.[6]

4. **Though the Preamble refers to the Baptist Faith and Message, it glaringly does not quote it.** Article IV is specifically mentioned but only in passing as expressing the authors' views in a "general way." I would have appreciated their engagement of paragraph A of that article, which states, "Regeneration, or the new birth, is a work of God's grace whereby believers become new creatures in Christ Jesus. It is a change of heart wrought by the Holy Spirit through conviction of sin, *to which* the sinner responds in repentance toward God and faith in the Lord Jesus Christ" (emphasis added). I will have more to say on this in Chapter 8 where I examine the TS statement on regeneration.

5. **The Preamble leaves one with the unmistakable impression that, despite disclaimers, Calvinism really is to be feared and resisted.** This sentence is the most egregious example: "Even the minority of Southern Baptists who have affiliated themselves as Calvinists generally modify its teachings in order to mitigate certain unacceptable conclusions (e.g., anti-missionism, hyper-Calvinism, double predestination, limited atonement, etc.)." Here the authors betray either their bias against or misunderstanding of historic Calvinism. Or both. Biblical Calvinism, or

[6] Rick Patrick has defended the legitimacy of using the "Traditional" language by appealing to the work of E.Y. Mullins, Herschel Hobbs, Adrian Rogers, Fisher Humphreys and Paul Robertson. His arguments are unconvincing. See https://theologicalmatters.com/2016/09/06/the-rise-of-soteriological-traditionalism/ [accessed February 5, 2018].

what Andrew Fuller called "strict Calvinism," needs no such modifications. Such terms as "anti-missionism" and "hyper-Calvinism" perpetuate the easily-debunked-but-never-dying myth that Calvinism undermines evangelism.

Any honest reading of history will show that many of the greatest evangelists and missionaries the world has ever seen have held firmly to the doctrines of grace. Calvinists do have variations with regard to reprobation vs. preterition and exactly how to articulate the accomplishment of the atonement (sufficient for all, efficient for the elect vs. sufficient only for the elect, etc.) but those are intramural theological debates—not attempts to "modify" Calvinism. Granted, there are self-described "modified Calvinists" who reject one or more of the so-called "five points" but nowhere does this Preamble appear to have such people in mind.

Furthermore, the authors seem to have forgotten the near apostasy of the SBC in the last quarter of the twentieth century. Consider the line of reasoning that the following statements reveal. "For almost a century, Southern Baptists have found that a sound, biblical soteriology can be taught, maintained, and defended without subscribing to Calvinism....Without ascribing [sic] to Calvinism, Southern Baptists have reached around the world with the Gospel message of salvation by grace alone through faith in Christ alone. Baptists have been well-served by a straightforward soteriology rooted in the fact that Christ is willing and able to save any and every sinner." This sounds as if the demise of Calvinism in the early part of the 20th century set the SBC's sails for smooth sailing doctrinally, evangelistically and missionally over the last

100 years. Anyone who lived as a Southern Baptist during the last two decades of the 20th century knows better. We almost reached a point of no return in our slide into neo-orthodoxy and liberalism. It should be noted that it was not on the Calvinists' watch that this happened. To suggest that all has been well doctrinally in the SBC Zion during the last 100 years ignores that dramatic, historic era in Southern Baptist life and simply distorts the documentable record.

6. **Finally, as I worked my way through the Preamble I could not help noticing what can be properly described as a paternalistic attitude.** The framers describe themselves and their phantom "Southern Baptist majority" as having fellowshipped "happily" with Calvinists "while kindly resisting Calvinism itself." Though less sanguine in their evaluation of "most Southern Baptist Calvinists" they nevertheless acknowledge that, "to their credit" those in this group "have not demanded the adoption of their view as the standard."This statement leaves me wondering who exactly is making such demands and what is the exact nature of such demands? Are Calvinists making threats? Or employing physical coercion? Or intimidation? The very next sentence, however, is the one that blatantly reveals a condescending attitude toward Southern Baptist Calvinists. "We would be fine if this consensus continued, but some New Calvinists seem to be pushing for a radical alteration of this longstanding arrangement." In other words, the authors and signers would be content ("fine") if Calvinists in the SBC would only maintain our supposedly minority status, being ever so grateful that "the majority" is willing "happily" to fellowship with us despite our theology, which that same "majority" so "kindly" re-

sists. As long as Calvinists stay in their assigned place and don't wander beyond their boundaries, then the authors "would be fine." Unfortunately, as I suspect the originators of this document know full well, the doctrines of God's grace in salvation are spreading rapidly not only within the SBC but beyond it as well. There is a doctrinal resurgence afoot and those who would be "fine" if Calvinists stayed in their assigned corner have become alarmed by continued growth of this movement.

4

Interacting with Article One

The Gospel

The framers of the TS offer 10 "Articles of Affirmation and Denial" in setting forth what they believe "most Southern Baptists" will find acceptable and true to the teachings of the Bible on the nature of salvation. Obviously, the articles should be understood as summary statements and not detailed explanations of the doctrinal positions asserted. An impressive array of Scripture citations follows each one. A suggestion that I would make to the authors and signers of the document is that they provide an additional document that includes exegesis of the texts cited. This would further promote understanding of their views and demonstrate the interpretive approach that has led them to their doctrinal positions. It would also provide opportunity for further dialogue by allowing those who differ with some of their positions to interact with their interpretation of Holy Scripture.

I will give my thoughts on each of the 10 articles, noting areas of agreement and elaborating the points of disagreement.

ARTICLE ONE: THE GOSPEL

We affirm that the Gospel is the good news that God has made a way of salvation through the life, death, and resurrection of the Lord Jesus Christ for any person. This is in keeping with God's desire for every person to be saved.

We deny that only a select few are capable of responding to the Gospel while the rest are predestined to an eternity in hell.

Genesis 3:15; Psalm 2:1–12; Ezekiel 18:23, 32; Luke 19.10; Luke 24:45–49; John 1:1–18, 3:16; Romans 1:1–6, 5:8; 8:34; 2 Corinthians 5:17–21; Galatians 4:4–7; Colossians 1:21–23; 1 Timothy 2:3–4; Hebrews 1:1–3; 4:14–16; 2 Peter 3:9

I also affirm that the gospel is good news that God has made a way of salvation through the person and work of Jesus though I think that statement stops short of declaring what the gospel *actually* is and does. I affirm that God has actually provided salvation for sinners through the life, death and resurrection of Jesus. The language of this article seems to lean away from an objective provision of salvation and toward a mere *potential* provision of a "way" of salvation. It is the difference between clearing a road in the jungle so that any who are lost may find their way home by it and actually going to those who are lost and bringing them home along the road. Jesus did not merely make salvation possible. He actually accomplished salvation by His life, death and resurrection.

Paul speaks in objective terms about the gospel when he defines it in 1 Corinthians 15:1–4 by asserting "that Christ died for our sins in accordance with the Scriptures, that he was buried, that he was raised on the third day in accordance with the Scriptures." "For our sins" indicates an objective accomplishment. Similarly, in Romans 1:16 Paul calls the gospel "the power of God for salvation to everyone who believes." Not potential power "for any person" (as article 1 states), but real power to all who believe. Certainly, "any person" who believes the gospel will be saved, though the article does not qualify their affirmation that way.

I can also affirm "God's desire for every person to be saved" though I suspect that my reasons for doing so would differ from those who have framed this document. In His law God commands everyone to have no other gods before Him (Exodus 20:3) and in His gospel He "commands all people everywhere to repent" (Acts 17:30). This revealed "desire" of God in no way mitigates His eternal purpose as expressed, regarding salvation, in the doctrine of unconditional election. This latter doctrine involves the "secret things that belong to the Lord our God" while the former "desire" is part of "the things that are revealed" which "belong to us and to our children" (Deuteronomy 29:29). God has revealed His will that all people be saved but He has purposed that His chosen people will infallibly be saved.

The denial seems to have in mind the following idea which I have never heard anyone assert as a conviction: that only a select few (the elect?) are capable of responding to the gospel while the rest are predestined to hell. Assuming that by "capable" the authors mean "the spiritual ability to repent and believe" (which is the only saving response to the gospel) then I think they have denied too little. Scripture teaches that no sinner has the innate ability to repent and believe the gospel. Jesus said, "No one *can* come to me unless the Father who sent me draws him. And I will raise him up on the last day" (John 6:44; cf. 6:65; emphasis added). Paul said, "the mind that is set on the flesh is hostile to God, for it does not submit to God's law; indeed, it *cannot*. Those who are in the flesh *cannot* please God." (Romans 8:7–8; emphasis added). Faith pleases God. "Can" (*dunatai*) is a word of ability. These verses teach that no unconverted person—regardless of whether he is predestined in any sense to any destination—has the spiritual ability to respond to the gospel by his own free will. This is at variance with the denial which necessarily implies everyone—and "not only a select few"—has the ability to repent and believe.

This first article signals the authors' and signers' understanding that the human will was not terribly affected by the fall. Their views on this are stated more plainly in Article Two.

5

Interacting with Article Two

The Sinfulness of Man

ARTICLE TWO: THE SINFULNESS OF MAN

We affirm that, because of the fall of Adam, every person inherits a nature and environment inclined toward sin and that every person who is capable of moral action will sin. Each person's sin alone brings the wrath of a holy God, broken fellowship with Him, ever-worsening selfishness and destructiveness, death, and condemnation to an eternity in hell.

We deny that Adam's sin resulted in the incapacitation of any person's free will or rendered any person guilty before he has personally sinned. While no sinner is remotely capable of achieving salvation through his own effort, we deny that any sinner is saved apart from a free response to the Holy Spirit's drawing through the Gospel.

Genesis 3:15–24; 6:5; Deuteronomy 1:39; Isaiah 6:5, 7:15–16;53:6; Jeremiah 17:5,9, 31:29–30; Ezekiel 18:19–20; Romans 1:18–32; 3:9–18, 5:12, 6:23; 7:9; Matthew 7:21–23; 1 Corinthians 1:18–25; 6:9–10;15:22; 2 Corinthians 5:10; Hebrews 9:27–28; Revelation 20:11–15

The affirmation reflects the authors' and signers appreciation of the 1963 revision of Article III in the original Baptist Faith and Message of 1925. When examined together, the significance of the revision is obvious.

1925 BF&M Article III:

He was created in a state of holiness under the law of his Maker, but, through the temptation of Satan, he transgressed the command of God and fell from his original holiness and righteousness; *whereby his posterity inherit a nature corrupt and in bondage to sin, are under condemnation, and as soon as they are capable of moral action, become actual transgressors* (emphasis added).

1963 BF&M Article III:

By his free choice man sinned against God and brought sin into the human race. Through the temptation of Satan man transgressed the command of God, and fell from his original innocence; *whereby his posterity inherit a nature and an environment inclined toward sin, and as soon as they are capable of moral action become transgressors and are under condemnation* (emphasis added).

The portion in italics highlights the change. In 1925 Southern Baptists acknowledged that Adam's sin left humanity with a corrupted nature that is "in bondage to sin" and also "under condemnation." The 1963 statement (which remains virtually unchanged at this point in the 2000 revision), reflecting the doctrinal downgrade of the SBC in that era that ultimately necessitated the conservative resurgence that began in the next decade, reduces the impact of the fall from leaving man's nature enslaved to sin to leaving it, along with his environment, "inclined toward sin" (Mark Coppenger addresses this in a helpful article documenting "The Ascent of Lost Man in Southern Baptist Preaching").[7] More significant is the removal in 1963 of the idea that people are, because of their inherited sinful nature, "under condemnation" (1925), though such culpability is acknowledged to be the case after they "become transgressors." This significant change cuts in half the authors' claim in the Preamble that their view of soteriology has been held by Southern Baptists for "almost a century."

As with many of the statements in these 10 Articles the first sentence of this affirmation is problematic not for what it says but for what it leaves unsaid. It is true that the fall has left people with a nature and environment "inclined toward sin" and that "every person who is capable of moral action will sin." But there is much, much more related to this that is true and that has historically been affirmed not only by Southern Baptists, but by Protestant orthodoxy in general. Rather than leave the point ambiguous, as the 1963 and 2000 BF&M do, the second sentence of the affirmation rejects a key point of that orthodoxy when it states that "each person's sin *alone* brings the wrath of a holy God…" (emphasis added).

The Second London Baptist Confession of Faith (published in1689, which is essentially the same as the 1742 Philadelphia Confession and the Charleston Confession of 1767) along with

[7] Mark Coppenger, "The Ascent of Lost Man in Southern Baptist Preaching" *The Founders Journal* 25 (Summer 1996), 5–21.

the Savoy Declaration (1658) and Westminster Confession (1646) all take a position that is contrary to the authors and signers of this statement.[8] In what is Article 6, paragraph 3 in each of those confessions the imputation of sin and guilt from Adam is asserted. The Baptist version is more elaborate than its Congregationalist and Presbyterian counterparts at this point:

> They [our first parents] being the root, and by God's appointment, standing in the room and stead of all mankind, the guilt of the sin was imputed, and corrupted nature conveyed, to all their posterity descending from them by ordinary generation, being now conceived in sin, and by nature children of wrath, the servants of sin, the subjects of death, and all other miseries, spiritual, temporal, and eternal, unless the Lord Jesus set them free.

Similarly, the first official confession of faith that Southern Baptists produced and which is still used at two of our seminaries, the Abstract of Principles, says that Adam's "posterity inherit a nature corrupt and wholly opposed to God and His law, are *under condemnation*, and as soon as they are capable of moral action, become actual transgressors" (emphasis added). I do not understand how anyone could, with integrity, sign this statement as well as this new document on "traditional" Baptist soteriology. At this point, they are mutually exclusive.

The authors and signers of the statement under review flatly reject the historic Southern Baptist position on sin as reflected in our earliest and most influential confessions. In fact, the second sentence of this Article Two's affirmation is actually much closer to the Mormon view of sin, which says, "We believe that men will be punished for their own sins, and not for Adam's

[8] See http://www.proginosko.com/docs/wcf_sdfo_lbcf.html

transgression." While no evangelical denies that sinners are guilty before God and liable to His wrath by virtue of their own sins, when the authors of this statement add the word "alone" to that point, they transgress the bounds of Protestant orthodoxy.

The key biblical text that must be considered at this point is Romans 5:12–19. Five times in this passage (12, 15, 17, 18, 19) the universal judgment of condemnation and death on all men is attributed to the one sin of the first man Adam. There is an undeniable solidarity between the first Adam and his posterity. Death is the penalty for sin and it has "spread to all men" (12) as an act of justice. Unless the penalty has been unjustly executed it is inescapable that all men are regarded guilty when the sentence is pronounced, which was at the point of Adam's sin. The last phrase of verse 12, when seen in the light of the whole passage, forcefully makes this point. Death spread to all men "because all sinned" (*ep ho pantes hamarton*). This raises the question, "How and when did all men sin?" The context gives the answer.

In verse 18 Paul clearly joins the sin of Adam to the condemnation of all men. Verse 19 identifies Adam's disobedience as the cause of many being "made" (*katestarthesan*) sinners. Adam's sin is constitutive of the sinfulness and condemnation of men. Universal judgment and death are inextricably bound to the sin of the original man in verses 15–19. The thematic integrity of the pericope indicates that Paul is dealing with the same issue in verse 12 that he considers in verses 15–19, namely, the origin of death and condemnation. In verse 12 he charges the death of all men to the sin of all men. In verses 15–19 he attributes death and condemnation to the sin of Adam.

In Paul's mind there is a union of some sort between the sin of Adam and the sin of all. Historically, Baptists like Andrew Fuller, Charles Spurgeon and R.B.C. Howell (following the

Second London Baptist Confession of Faith) have argued that this relationship is rooted in the federal union of Adam to the human race. Because he is the representative of the race, Adam's sin is imputed to all his offspring. We are not sinners because we sin; rather, we sin because we are sinners.

The statement of denial is one of the most problematic in the whole document. I have tried to understand, from the texts cited, how the authors and signers have concluded that there is no "incapacitation of any person's free will" as a result of the fall. Our Lord's statement that "no one can come to me unless the Father who sent me draws him' (John 6:44, cf. v. 65) and that of the Apostle Paul that the mind that is set on the flesh "cannot" submit to God's law or please God (Romans 8:7–8) clearly teach that there is an inability on the part of natural men to come to Christ or repent and believe. What do such statements mean if not that sin has resulted in an incapacitation of the will?

Furthermore, it is strange to find this deterministic statement in Article Two's affirmation: "every person who is capable of moral action will sin." What is the source or power of such inevitability? Adam lived for a while without sinning. Is it not then possible that someone might live—at least for a little while—without sin? The dilemma that I suspect the authors are trying to avoid by their protection of a libertarian free will that is in no way incapacitated by the fall is not resolved by their ironically deterministic language.

This article also raises questions about the roots of the authors' and signers' theological convictions. The self-described "Classical Arminian" and highly respected Roger Olson has weighed in at this point raising serious concerns about their denial "that Adam's sin resulted in the incapacitation of any person's free will or rendered any person guilty before he has personally sinned."[9] Olson gave a glowing review to the book, *Whosoever Will: A Biblical-Theological Critique of Five-Point Calvinism*,[10] which was edited and written by many of the promoters of this statement. His concerns, therefore, come as one who is very sympathetic to the theology of many of the advocates of this document and should be weighed heavily.

> A classical Arminian would never deny that Adam's sin resulted in the incapacitation of any person's free will. Classical Arminianism (as I have demonstrated in *Arminian Theology: Myths and Realities*) strongly affirms the bondage of the will to sin before and apart from prevenient grace's liberating work.
>
> Now, perhaps this is the point of the statement's mention of "the Holy Spirit's drawing through the Gospel." But that, too, can be interpreted in a semi-Pelagian way. Semi-Pelagians such as Philip Limborch and (at least in some of his writings) Charles Finney affirmed the necessity of the gospel and the Holy Spirit's enlightening work through it for salvation. What made them semi-Pelagian was their denial or neglect of the divine initiative in salvation (except the gospel message).
>
> The problem with this Southern Baptist statement is its neglect of emphasis on the necessity of the prevenience of supernatural grace for the exercise of a good will toward God

[9] http://www.patheos.com/blogs/rogereolson/2012/06/thoughts-about-"a-statement-of-the-traditional-southern-baptist-understanding-of-gods-plan-of-salvation-"/

[10] The review is published on the website, Baptist Theology, which is owned and operated by Southwestern Baptist Theological Seminary, http://www.baptisttheology.org/book-reviews/whosoever-will/ [accessed February 6, 2018].

> (including acceptance of the gospel by faith). If the authors believe in that cardinal biblical truth, they need to spell it out more clearly. And they need to delete the sentence that denies the incapacitation of free will due to Adam's sin.
>
> Leaving the statement as it stands, without a clear affirmation of the bondage of the will to sin apart from supernatural grace, inevitably hands the Calvinists ammunition to use against non-Calvinist Baptists.
>
> It doesn't matter what "most Baptists" believe or what is the "traditional Southern Baptist understanding." For a long time I've been stating that most American Christians, including most Baptists, are semi-Pelagian, not Arminian and not merely non-Calvinist.
>
> Calvinists and Arminians stand together, with Scripture, against semi-Pelagianism. (Romans 3:11 and 1 Corinthians 4:7 to name just two passages.)[11]

I fear that Olson may be correct in his evaluation that "most American Christians, including most Baptists, are semi-Pelagian." This concern is also shared by Al Mohler who has written, "Some portions of the statement actually go beyond Arminianism and appear to affirm semi-Pelagian understandings of sin, human nature, and the human will—understandings that virtually all Southern Baptists have denied."[12] My hope and prayer are that the Southern Baptist brothers who have signed on to this statement will rethink what they are saying and of-

[11] http://www.patheos.com/blogs/rogereolson/2012/06/thoughts-about-"a-statement-of-the-traditional-southern-baptist-understanding-of-gods-plan-of-salvation-"/

[12] https://albertmohler.com/2012/06/06/southern-baptists-and-salvation-its-time-to-talk [accessed February 6, 2018].

fer clarifications if not retractions that show they are indeed in step not only with "traditional" Southern Baptist understanding but also historic, orthodox Protestant understanding, and even more importantly, with biblical teaching regarding the nature of sin and the fall.

6

Interacting with Article Three

The Atonement of Christ

ARTICLE THREE: THE ATONEMENT OF CHRIST

We affirm that the penal substitution of Christ is the only available and effective sacrifice for the sins of every person.

We deny that this atonement results in salvation without a person's free response of repentance and faith. We deny that God imposes or withholds this atonement without respect to an act of the person's free will. We deny that Christ died only for the sins of those who will be saved.

Psalm 22:1–31; Isaiah 53:1–12; John 12:32, 14:6; Acts 10:39–43; Acts 16:30–32; Romans 3:21–26; 2 Corinthians 5:21; Galatians 3:10–14; Philippians 2:5–11; Colossians 1:13–20; 1 Timothy 2:5–6; Hebrews 9:12–15, 24–28; 10:1–18; 1 John 1:7; 2:2

I appreciate the claims of exclusivity and efficacy that are made for the atonement in this article along with its affirmation of penal substitution. I also agree with the first sentence of the denial. No one is saved without responding (to the gospel) with repentance and faith. Beyond these points of agreement, however, I find some of the language confusing and imprecise and simply disagree with the authors on what actually happened when Jesus died on the cross.

The positive affirmation makes two claims for the penal substitution of Christ: 1) it is "the only available... sacrifice for the sins of every person" and 2) it is "the only... effective sacrifice for the sins of every person." The exclusivity of Christ as the only Savior that anyone in the world has available is an important point to express in this day of ideological pluralism and theological inclusivism. Acts 4:12 and 1 Timothy 2:5–6 plainly teach this. But the statement clearly means to say more than this.

By coupling "effective" with "available," the article affirms that Christ has effectively provided a penal, substitutionary atonement for "the sins of every person." In other words, this statement affirms universal atonement—that Christ actually paid for the sins of every person. The first sentence of the denial shows how the signers avoid actual universalism (the belief that everyone will be saved) because it states that the effective sacrifice (atonement) will not result in salvation "without a person's free response of repentance and faith." While I am glad for this rejection of universalism, I am left wondering what exactly is the nature of the atonement's efficacy. In what sense is the penal substitution of Christ an "effective sacrifice for the sins of every person" if it does not effectively (actually) save? Would you call a mission "effective" that did not accomplish what it claimed to accomplish? I wouldn't. I would say its effectiveness was limited by the response of the people for whom it was intended.

The debate over the extent of the atonement has a long history among evangelical Christians. The Baptist Faith and Message allows room for both the Calvinistic and Arminian view of atonement when it states in article II that "in His substitutionary death on the cross He [Jesus] made provision for the redemption of men from sin." I have no illusions that in this little book I will be able to convince the proponents of universal atonement that what Christ accomplished on the cross was objective, definite and intended actually to save particular sinners rather than merely make salvation possible for all sinners. What I would like to point out, however, is that everyone "limits" or particularizes the atonement in some way, unless true universalism is affirmed. Either the atoning work of Jesus is limited in its scope—that is, intended only for particular people, or it is limited in its efficacy—that is, not able to save the very people for whom it was intended.

The framers of this document have plainly declared themselves to be in the latter camp. While asserting that the death of Christ is "an effective sacrifice for every sin of every person" they go on to deny that it actually saves every sinner. They have a purportedly "effective" sacrifice that does not actually save some of the people for whom it was made. Their view of Christ's atonement limits its power.

In John 10:11 Jesus describes himself as "the good shepherd" who "lays down his life for his sheep." He later says to the Jews who were around him, "You do not believe because you are not part of my flock" (John 10:26). In John 6:38–39 Jesus says that He came to do the Father's will, "and this is the will of him who sent me, that I should lose nothing of all that he has given me, but raise it up on the last day." All that Jesus was entrusted to do—including His atoning work on the cross—was to be effectually accomplished. The question must be asked then, "Did Jesus do the Father's will?" "Was He successful in his mission?" I believe that He was and that this is exactly what He meant when He said from the cross, "It is finished!"

Wisdom from Spurgeon on this point might be helpful. In his sermon entitled, "Particular Redemption" (#181), he made the following remarks.

> All Christians hold that Christ died to redeem, but all Christians do not teach the same Redemption! We differ as to the nature of Atonement and as to the design of Redemption. For instance, the Arminian holds that Christ, when He died, did not die with an intent to save any particular person. And they teach that Christ's death does not, in itself, secure beyond doubt the salvation of any man living. They believe that Christ died to make the salvation of all men possible, or that by the doing of something else, any man who pleases may attain unto eternal life! Consequently, they are obliged to hold that if man's will would not give way and voluntarily surrender to Divine Grace, then Christ's Atonement would be worthless! They hold that there was no particularity and specialty in the death of Christ. Christ died, according to them, as much for Judas in Hell as for Peter who mounted to Heaven! They believe that for those who are consigned to eternal fire, there was as true and real a Redemption made as for those who now stand before the Throne of the Most High! Now we believe no such thing! We hold that Christ, when He died, had an objective in view and that objective will most assuredly and beyond a doubt, be accomplished! We measure the design of Christ's death by the effect of it. If anyone asks us, "What did Christ design to do by His death?" We answer that question by asking him another—"What has Christ done, or what will Christ do by His death?" We declare that the measure of the

effect of Christ's love is the measure of the design of it! We cannot so belie our reason as to think that the intention of Almighty God could be frustrated or that the design of so great a thing as the Atonement can by any way whatever, be missed of. We hold—we are not afraid to say what we believe—that Christ came into this world with the intention of saving "a multitude which no man can number." And we believe that as the result of this, every person for whom He died must, beyond the shadow of a doubt, be cleansed from sin and stand, washed in His blood, before the Father's Throne. We do not believe that Christ made any effectual Atonement for those who are forever damned! We dare not think that the blood of Christ was ever shed with the intention of saving those whom God foreknew would never be saved—and some of whom were even in Hell when Christ, according to some men's account, died to save them!...

Now, beloved, when you hear any one laughing or jeering at a limited atonement, you may tell him this. General atonement is like a great wide bridge with only half an arch; it does not go across the stream: it only professes to go half way; it does not secure the salvation of anybody. Now, I had rather put my foot upon a bridge as narrow as Hungerford, which went all the way across, than on a bridge that was as wide as the world, if it did not go all the way across the stream.

While the authors of the document do not want to be described as Arminians, and I want to honor that desire, their view of the atonement does have more in common with Arminianism (as Spurgeon illustrates) than with the understanding of the churches and leaders who founded the Southern Baptist Convention in 1845.

The second sentence of the denial highlights two of the issues that are a recurring problem for me in this document: "We deny that God imposes or withholds this atonement without respect to an act of the person's free will." First, beyond the whole of "Article Eight: The Free Will of Man," the entire document seems to be more concerned to protect the integrity of man's free will than to defend the glory of God. In fact, one will search in vain for any reference to the glory of God in the Preamble or Articles. Obviously, this does not mean that the authors and signers have no regard for the glory of God, but it does suggest how out of alignment with the great emphasis of Scripture their thinking is at this point.

I cannot imagine the Apostle Paul submitting for public review his understanding of salvation while failing to emphasize, much less mention, the glory of the God who saves. A cursory reading of his symphony on salvation by grace in Ephesians 1:4–14 underscores this.

> He chose us in him before the foundation of the world…he predestined us for adoption through Jesus Christ according to the purpose of his will, *to the praise of his glorious grace*…7 In him we have redemption through his blood…11 [and] have been predestined according to the purpose of him who works all things according to the counsel of his will, 12 so that we who were the first to hope in Christ might be *to the praise of his glory*…[and we have been] 13 sealed with the promised Holy Spirit…14 *to the praise of his glory*" (emphasis added).

The second recurring concern that I have with the document is what seems to be a confusing of categories and imprecise language. For example, where in Scripture do we read of God ever "imposing or withholding" atonement from someone? "God put [Jesus] forward as a propitiation by his blood" (Romans 3:25). "He himself bore our sins in his body on the tree" (1 Peter 2:24). These two verses are representative of the whole New Testament's teaching that the atoning work of Jesus on the cross is finished. It happened. It is the accomplishment of salvation.

I could possibly understand speaking of God "imposing or withholding" salvation, or even more specifically, forgiveness, from someone. Paul even entertains the prospect that God might withhold repentance from some who oppose the ministry of the gospel in the church (2 Timothy 2:25). But to use such language when speaking of the atonement is confusing. It does, however, highlight one reason that I believe theological discussion in general and regarding salvation in particular can be difficult to engage profitably. We need to have a careful definition of terms and make sure that we are reading out of the same dictionary. To the degree that we can do that with biblical, theological and historical terminology, mutual understanding will be promoted.

7

Interacting with Article Four

The Grace of God

ARTICLE FOUR: THE GRACE OF GOD

We affirm that grace is God's generous decision to provide salvation for any person by taking all of the initiative in providing atonement, in freely offering the Gospel in the power of the Holy Spirit, and in uniting the believer to Christ through the Holy Spirit by faith.

We deny that grace negates the necessity of a free response of faith or that it cannot be resisted. We deny that the response of faith is in any way a meritorious work that earns salvation.

Ezra 9:8; Proverbs 3:34; Zechariah 12:10; Matthew 19:16–30, 23:37; Luke 10:1–12; Acts 15:11; 20:24; Romans 3:24, 27–28; 5:6, 8, 15–21; Galatians 1:6; 2:21; 5; Ephesians 2:8–10; Philippians 3:2–9; Colossians 2:13–17; Hebrews 4:16; 9:28; 1 John 4:19

I find the statements in this article more confusing than theologically problematic. Given the accomplishments and prominence of the authors and promoters of this document I readily admit that the confusion could be completely due to my inability to keep up with their biblical and theological thinking. Regardless of where the fault lies, I, for one, would greatly benefit from some exegetical explanation of this affirmation and denial. Carefully reading through the proof texts cited does not help me understand this article which they supposedly support.

If I take the affirmation as generically affirming the grace of God in providing salvation then I can say a hearty, "Amen." It is when I read the affirmation slowly, and focus on the clauses and their connections (something that a public statement like this deserves) that the fog starts rising in my understanding.

My understanding of grace has been shaped by those biblical passages that speak of it in terms of God's activity and provision. I can't recall the Bible speaking of it as His "decision" (though certainly if God acts or provides, it is because He decided to act or provide). This is how I read Ephesians 2:8, "By grace you have been saved through faith. And this is not your own doing; it is the gift of God." The grace by which we have been saved is God's saving work in Christ. It has come to us undeserved and without our effort and is personified in Jesus Himself, who is full of grace and truth (John 1:14).

I am not suggesting that the authors and signers of this statement would disagree with any of this. They just didn't state it. What they do state is that grace is God's "decision to provide salvation to any person by taking all of the initiative" in three specific areas: 1) "in providing atonement," 2) "in freely offering the Gospel in the power of the Holy Spirit," 3) "in uniting the believer to Christ through the Holy Spirit by faith."

Consider what each of these clauses asserts.

1. Though the first of these assertions strikes me as an awkward way to say it and perhaps stops short of saying enough, who can question God's initiative "in providing atonement?" He certainly took "all the initiative" in providing atonement by sending Jesus into the world.

2. The second assertion is more difficult to understand. Where in the Bible do we read of God taking initiative "in freely offering the gospel?" Believers are called to proclaim the gospel (Matthew 28:19–20) and the New Testament certainly records examples of first-century Christians doing just that "in the power of the Holy Spirit" (Acts 2:1–41; 4:8–12; 7:1–60, etc.). Perhaps 2 Corinthians 5:20 might lend some credence to this language, but there Paul speaks of God using Christians as his ambassadors, making an appeal through them as they themselves implore unbelievers to be reconciled to God. Besides, the authors obviously did not have this verse in mind since it is not included in their proof texts for this article. To speak of God offering the gospel "in the power of the Holy Spirit" may not be contrary to Scripture, but it strikes me as an odd affirmation to make on a such thin exegetical foundation.

3. The third clause is much more understandable and, though I could quibble over a simpler way to say it, the Bible certainly teaches that God takes all of the initiative in uniting believers to Christ. It also clearly teaches that such union comes through faith and only by the ministry of the Holy Spirit.

The denial seems to be aimed at the unfortunate phrase, "irresistible grace," that is represented by the fourth letter in the acrostic TULIP. Some people have misunderstood that point as teaching that Calvinists see God's grace operating in such a way that people are dragged, kicking and screaming, into a saving relationship with Christ. Of course, that is hardly the case and no respected Calvinistic teacher has ever advocated God's grace operating in such a manner. Since the real issue at stake is better addressed in terms of God's effectual call, I will reserve further comments for my response to article eight, which denies the existence of effectual calling.

The final sentence of the denial is a statement that strikes me as eminently biblical and I am grateful to see the idea that faith is a meritorious work rejected so plainly.

8

Interacting with Article Five

The Regeneration of the Sinner

ARTICLE FIVE: THE REGENERATION OF THE SINNER

We affirm that any person who responds to the Gospel with repentance and faith is born again through the power of the Holy Spirit. He is a new creation in Christ and enters, at the moment he believes, into eternal life.

We deny that any person is regenerated prior to or apart from hearing and responding to the Gospel.

Luke 15:24; John 3:3; 7:37–39; 10:10; 16:7–14; Acts 2:37–39; Romans 6:4–11; 10:14; 1 Corinthians 15:22; 2 Corinthians 5:17; Galatians 2:20; 6:15; Colossians 2:13; 1 Peter 3:18

This statement seems to affirm a synergistic understanding of regeneration. That is, it seems to affirm that regeneration is a cooperative effort between an unbeliever and God. The reason I say "*seems* to affirm" is due to imprecise language which, when engaging in theological dialogue is always problematic.

The phrase, "any person who responds to the Gospel with repentance and faith is born again through the power of the Holy Spirit," can be taken two ways. It can mean, "any person who responds to the Gospel does so because he is a born again person." Or it can mean, as I suspect the authors mean, "any person who responds to the Gospel is by that response born again." The difference in the possible meanings can be illustrated by the following two sentences: "Anyone who lifts 500 pounds is strong" vs. "Anyone who passes the bar exam is an attorney."

Given the whole statement in which this Article Five appears, as well as some of the defenses that have been offered by prominent signers and defenders of the statement, I am confident that those who originated and are promoting it do want to affirm that responding to the gospel with repentance and faith is what makes a person born again. As I have already noted, this is synergistic regeneration.

In the interest of clarity, let me note that when "synergism" vs. "monergism" is discussed in Calvinism/Arminianism debates what typically is in view is regeneration. The two words are theological shorthand to describe two opposing views of how regeneration comes to a person. Monergism sees regeneration to be a sovereign work of God in which He alone is active—that He gives new birth without any cooperative effort on the part of the individual. Synergism teaches that God regenerates a person only if and after that person repents and believes.

This issue highlights the importance of exercising care and precision when discussing fine points of biblical theology. If we move beyond the realm of regeneration into sanctification then nearly all monergists (with regard to regeneration) are synergists. That is, they believe that while there is no cooperation on the part of the individual in securing his new birth there is cooperative effort on his part in securing his growth in grace or sanctification.

With that said, the affirmers' apparent synergistic view of regeneration is biblically untenable as well as being in violation of the plain reading of Article IV of the Baptist Faith and Message (BF&M) statement of the Southern Baptist Convention, as noted below.

I must confess that I do not understand the rationale for the inclusion of most of the proof texts that are attached to this article and I am left wondering how their exegesis even touches on, much less supports, the authors' and signers' synergistic understanding of the new birth. These passages include obviously important and vitally connected issues: the necessity of the new birth, the necessity of the work of the Spirit in regeneration, the instrumentality of the Word of truth in regeneration, the necessity of repentance and faith, that there are operations of the Spirit that continue in the believer's life beyond regeneration, that regeneration is likened to a new creation, that regeneration is the new covenant fulfillment of the type of circumcision; but none of the proof texts indicate that regeneration is suspended on and dependent on the prior exhibition of repentance and faith on the part of the sinner. It was also interesting that one of the classic passages on the method of the new birth is completely omitted.

That passage, however, deserves consideration. John 1:12–13 states, "But to all who did receive him, who believed in his name, he gave the right to become children of God, [13] who were born, not of blood nor of the will of the flesh nor of the will of man, but of God." Verse 12 teaches that those who receive Christ were authorized to become children of God—adopted into his family. Verse 13 explains how that happened by speaking of the act of birth—an act that will be elaborated in John 3:1–8. Those who are adopted into God's family entered into that privileged status because they believed. They believed because they had been born (again) wholly and exclusively by the work of God. John specifically and plainly denies that their spiritual birth came through their genealogy ("not of blood") or through the exercise of their own will ("the will of the flesh") or through the imposition of another's will ("nor of the will of man"). Rather, those who are children of God enter into that status because they have been monergistically "born…of God." So in terms of the application of salvation, this passage teaches that it flows like this: new birth—faith—adoption. It is impossible to reconcile synergistic regeneration with these verses.

This Johannine view of the operation of the Spirit in the new birth finds reinforcement in this statement found in his first letter, "Everyone who believes that Jesus is the Christ has been born of God" (1 John 5:10). John's pattern of argument throughout this whole letter is to give evidences of the new birth and not to prescribe its cause (2:29; 3:9, 10; 4:7; 5:4, 5). The whole letter teaches that the new birth is sovereignly given and is the fountain from which all spiritual life, including saving faith, flows.

This point is even more starkly taught by Jesus when he instructs Nicodemus in John 3. The Lord tells him "Truly, truly, I say to you, unless one is born again he cannot see the kingdom of God" (v. 3) and "Truly, truly, I say to you, unless one is born of water and the Spirit, he cannot [remember, "can" is a word of ability] enter the kingdom of God" (v. 5). Entrance into the kingdom is reserved for those who trust Christ. Jesus plainly states that such entrance is impossible unless one is born of the

Spirit. In fact, He goes even further by saying that not only is it impossible to enter the kingdom of God without being born again, one cannot even *see* the kingdom of God without this supernatural change.

When Nicodemus expresses incredulity over this teaching, Jesus includes in His response this astounding affirmation of the free will of the sovereign Spirit. "The wind blows where it wishes, and you hear its sound, but you do not know where it comes from or where it goes. So it is with everyone who is born of the Spirit" (v. 8). One of the concerns I have about this whole statement of affirmations and denials, as I have written previously, is the authors' apparent determination to protect the absolute freedom of fallen man's human will. Jesus shows a similar determination here, but it is directed toward the free will of God's Spirit in the work of regeneration. Like the wind, in granting new birth, the Spirit, "blows where [he] wishes."

Even without going into the point of the analogy of birth these passages are sufficiently clear to show that the Bible teaches that God works monergistically to grant new birth to sinners. That does not mean that a person is passive in salvation because salvation consists of much more than regeneration. It does mean, however, that it is God's will and God's action alone that brings about new birth. This is precisely what is confessed in Article IV of the BF&M.

That article reads in part,

> Salvation involves the redemption of the whole man, and is offered freely to all who accept Jesus Christ as Lord and Saviour, who by His own blood obtained eternal redemption for the believer. In its broadest sense salvation includes regeneration, justification, sanctification, and glorification. There is no salvation apart from personal faith in Jesus Christ as Lord.

> Regeneration, or the new birth, is a work of God's grace whereby believers become new creatures in Christ Jesus. It is a change of heart wrought by the Holy Spirit through conviction of sin, to which the sinner responds in repentance toward God and faith in the Lord Jesus Christ. Repentance and faith are inseparable experiences of grace.

This statement on regeneration affirms monergism. It is called a "work of God's grace" and "a change of heart wrought by the Holy Spirit." God alone is credited with being the Actor in the work of regeneration. Furthermore, the human action of repentance and faith are described as responsive. Ask any English professor to identify the antecedent of the pronoun "which" and he or she will tell you that it is the "It" that begins the sentence, which itself refers back to "Regeneration, or new birth." In other words, regeneration "is a change of heart... *to which the sinner responds in repentance... and faith*" (emphasis added).

The Baptist Faith and Message teaches the priority of regeneration to faith. Rather than faith resulting in the new birth (which would be like Jesus saying, "you cannot believe unless you enter the kingdom of God") the new birth results in faith. This is why the BF&M goes on to confess that "repentance and faith are inseparable experiences of *grace*" (emphasis added).

Not only are the authors and signers of this "Statement of the Traditional Southern Baptist Understanding of God's Plan of Salvation" out of step with Scripture in their view of regeneration, they are also out of step with the Baptist Faith and Message.[13]

[13] For a more complete statement on my understanding of regeneration see Tom Ascol, "Regeneration," *The Founders Journal* 34 (Fall 1998), 8–13.

9

INTERACTING WITH ARTICLE SIX
THE ELECTION TO SALVATION

ARTICLE SIX: THE ELECTION TO SALVATION

We affirm that, in reference to salvation, election speaks of God's eternal, gracious, and certain plan in Christ to have a people who are His by repentance and faith.

We deny that election means that, from eternity, God predestined certain people for salvation and others for condemnation.

Genesis 1:26–28; 12:1–3; Exodus 19:6; Jeremiah 31:31–33; Matthew 24:31; 25:34; John 6:70; 15:16; Romans 8:29–30, 33;9:6–8; 11:7; 1 Corinthians 1:1–2; Ephesians 1:4–6; 2:11–22; 3:1–11; 4:4–13; 1 Timothy 2:3–4; 1 Peter 1:1–2; 1 Peter 2:9; 2 Peter 3:9; Revelation 7:9–10

The lack of precision in the affirmation of this article makes its meaning ambiguous. The words "eternal, gracious, and certain" reflect emphases that the Bible itself makes regarding the doctrine of election. For example, Paul writes, God "chose us in him *before the foundation of the world.... In love* he predestined us for adoption..." (Ephesians 1:4–5, emphasis added). But unlike Paul, the authors of this statement reduce election to the devising of a "plan" by God "to have a people who are His by repentance and faith" rather than the actual choice of people to be "holy and blameless before him" (Ephesians 1:4). The Baptist Faith and Message 2000 speaks of election as God's "purpose" rather than his "plan." Article IV says,

> Election is the gracious purpose of God, according to which He regenerates, justifies, sanctifies, and glorifies sinners. It is consistent with the free agency of man, and comprehends all the means in connection with the end. It is the glorious display of God's sovereign goodness, and is infinitely wise, holy, and unchangeable. It excludes boasting and promotes humility.

It seems that the authors of the affirmation are following the late Herschel Hobbs who said of these verses, "Paul says that God elected a plan of salvation." I disagree with Hobbs at this point because the object of "chose" (*exelexato*) in verse 4 is "us"—people, believers—not a plan. Hobbs further described election as a fence that God set up, determining that only those who are "in Christ" will be saved. Again, the problem I have with this view is not that I disagree that God has purposed to save people "in Christ." Rather, my problem is grammatical. God is the subject of Paul's sentence. "Chose" is the verb. "Us" is the object. My view of inspiration will not allow me to deviate from the plain meaning of this plain statement. The object of election is people, not a plan.

It may be that the authors and signers of this statement do not agree with Hobbs, however. Perhaps they are affirming that election is God's choice to have for His people whoever repents and believes. This leaves one wondering if they are elect because they repent and believe or do they repent and believe because they are elect. Though I suspect that they mean the former, it is hard to know exactly because the statement is imprecise.

The denial is less ambiguous though it still leaves much to be desired with regard to clarity and simplicity. Here is what is obvious: they deny that God predestines anyone to heaven or hell. It is not uncommon to find references to "double predestination" when addressing this issue. In one sense the doctrine of unconditional election cannot escape its corresponding implication that if some are predestined to be saved then those who are not predestined to be saved are in some sense predestined to remain lost. Of course, this fact becomes an easy target for those who choose to do theology by caricature.

Typically, the misrepresentation goes something like this: "Calvinists believe that in eternity past God chose to send certain people to heaven and chose to send certain people to hell." Contrast this to the carefully worded statement from the Philadelphia Baptist Confession of Faith of 1742,

> By the decree of God, for the manifestation of His glory, some men and angels are predestinated, or foreordained to eternal life through Jesus Christ, to the praise of his glorious grace; others being left to act in their sin to their just condemnation, to the praise of his glorious justice (chapter 3, paragraph 3).

Note the lack of symmetry in the way that God's eternal decree is described. He positively, actively, predestines some to eternal life while others are simply "left to act in their sin and just condemnation." In other words (without going too deeply into the lapsarian question), in eternity past, when God chose particular sinners to be saved, He did not regard them as neutral or righteous, but as fallen and sinful. As such, election is the beginning of His rescue mission. It is His first step in His work to insure the salvation of sinners. He does not act in a symmetrical way with those whom He does not elect. That is, He does not "elect them to hell." They are already on the way to hell. God simply leaves them "to act in their sin to their just condemnation." This act of "non-election" is properly called preterition.

This is the way that the Bible teaches election. "But we ought always to give thanks to God for you, brothers beloved by the Lord, because God chose you as the firstfruits to be saved, through sanctification by the Spirit and belief in the truth" (2 Thessalonians 2:13). Jesus says, "All that the Father gives me will come to me, and whoever comes to me I will never cast out" (John 6:37). Again, it is important to deal honestly with the grammar of God's inerrant Word. God is always the subject and people are always the objects of election. Though I can think of two references in Scripture that could be taken to suggest that God intentionally fashioned some people for hell (Romans 9:22–23 and 1 Peter 2:8), the overwhelming emphasis is on His positive initiative to choose particular people to be saved.

This is why many shorter Baptist confessions only speak of election as the positive choice of God to rescue particular sinners through the provision of the gospel and operation of the Spirit. For example, the first confession that Southern Baptists ever produced, the Abstract of Principles of 1858 (which, by the way, every professor at Southern Seminary and Southeastern Seminary is contractually bound to teach in accordance with and not contrary to), states in Article V,

> Election is God's eternal choice of some persons unto everlasting life—not because of foreseen merit in them, but of his mere mercy in Christ—in consequence of which choice they are called, justified and glorified.

Or consider the New Hampshire Baptist Confession of 1833, which is the confessional foundation on which the Baptist Faith and Message, in all of its iterations, is built.

> We believe that Election is the eternal purpose of God, according to which he graciously regenerates, sanctifies, and saves sinners; that being perfectly consistent with the free agency of man, it comprehends all the means in connection with the end; that it is a most glorious display of God's sovereign goodness, being infinitely free, wise, holy, and unchangeable; that it utterly excludes boasting, and promotes humility, love, prayer, praise, trust in God, and active imitation of his free mercy; that it encourages the use of means in the highest degree; that it may be ascertained by its effects in all who truly believe the gospel; that it is the foundation of Christian assurance; and that to ascertain it with regard to ourselves demands and deserves the utmost diligence.

These three traditional Baptist confessions of faith (and this number could have been easily multiplied in this article) stand in stark contrast to the statement offered by those who would like to be thought of as representing the "traditional" Baptist understanding of salvation. Let's allow the first Southern Baptist theologian who produced a systematic theology textbook have the final say on this subject. John L. Dagg's *Manual of Theology* is worth reading, especially Book 7, chapter 4, section 1, from which the quote below is extracted.

> Those who are not included in the election of grace, are called, in Scripture, "the rest,"[Romans 11:7] and vessels of

wrath."[Romans 9:22] Why they are not included, we are as unable to explain as why the others are included; and we are therefore compelled to refer the matter to the sovereignty of God, who, beyond all doubt, acts herein most wisely and righteously, though he has not explained to us the reasons of his procedure. His absolute sovereignty, in the discrimination which he makes, is expressed by Paul in these words: "He hath mercy on whom he will have mercy; and whom he will he hardeneth."[Romans 9:18] The natural tendency of human depravity is such, that the heart grows harder under the general mercies which God bestows, unless he superadds to all the other benefits which he confers, the renewing grace of the Holy Spirit, by which the heart is changed. This renewing grace he gives or withholds at his sovereign pleasure. This sovereignty, in so bestowing mercy as to soften the hard heart, is unquestionably taught by the words just quoted, however we may interpret the phrase "he hardeneth." It is not necessary to understand these words as implying a positive act of God, exerted for the purpose of producing hardness of heart, and directed to this end. When Paul speaks of the vessels of mercy, he says that God hath "afore prepared" them for glory; but when he speaks of the vessels of wrath, as fitted for destruction, he does not say that God has fitted them for this end.[Romans 9:22, 23] As the potter, out of the same mass, makes one vessel to honor and another to dishonor;[Romans 9:21] so God, out of the same mass of mankind, prepares some for glory, as vessels of mercy; while others, whatever benefits they may receive from him, being left without renewing grace, abuse the mercies which he bestows, and, growing harder by the influence of their natural depravity, are vessels of wrath fitted for destruction.[14]

[14] John L. Dagg, *Manual of Theology* (South Carolina: Southern Baptist Publication Society, 1857; reprint, Harrisonburg, VA: Gano Books, 1990), 313–314.

10

Interacting with Article Seven

The Sovereignty of God

ARTICLE SEVEN: THE SOVEREIGNTY OF GOD

We affirm God's eternal knowledge of and sovereignty over every person's salvation or condemnation.

We deny that God's sovereignty and knowledge require Him to cause a person's acceptance or rejection of faith in Christ.

Genesis 1:1; 6:5–8; 18:16–33; 22; 2 Samuel 24:13–14; 1 Chronicles 29:10–20; 2 Chronicles 7:14; Joel 2:32; Psalm 23; 51:4; 139:1–6; Proverbs 15:3; John 6:44; Romans 11:3; Titus 3:3–7; James 1:13–15; Hebrews 11:6, 12:28; 1 Peter 1:17

The affirmation acknowledges truths about God that are essential to biblical Christianity while the denial raises questions about the authors' and signers' understanding of those truths. Once again, I find the wording uncharacteristically awkward for a public theological statement.

God certainly has "eternal knowledge" and "sovereignty" that extend to "every person's salvation or condemnation." The Baptist Faith and Message 2000 states the same truth more clearly in Article II.

> There is one and only one living and true God. He is an intelligent, spiritual, and personal Being, the Creator, Redeemer, Preserver, and Ruler of the universe. God is infinite in holiness and all other perfections. God is all powerful and all knowing; and His perfect knowledge extends to all things, past, present, and future [which would include "every person's salvation or condemnation], including the future decisions of His free creatures.

I am convinced that the Bible teaches both God's meticulous sovereignty and His exhaustive knowledge, including foreknowledge. Jesus encouraged His disciples by reminding them that God rules and overrules in even the most apparently insignificant events. "Are not two sparrows sold for a cent? And yet not one of them will fall to the ground apart from your Father" (Matthew 11:29, NASB). The point is that if God is that meticulously involved in small events then He can be trusted to rule sovereingly in every aspect of our lives. Similarly, the Lord spoke through Isaiah saying, "Remember this and stand firm, recall it to mind, you transgressors, remember the former things of old; for I am God, and there is no other; I am God, and there is none like me, declaring the end from the beginning and from ancient times things not yet done, saying, 'My counsel shall stand, and I will accomplish all my purpose,' calling a bird of prey from the east, the man of my counsel from a far country. I have spoken, and I will bring it to pass; I have purposed, and I will do it" (Isaiah 46:8–11). The ability to declare "the end from the beginning" necessitates unlimited knowledge, which God most certainly has.

The authors and signers may well believe all of this, too, but they did not affirm it. A theological affirmation that addresses God's sovereignty and knowledge should, like the BF&M does, include simple, clear statements about such matters.

The language used in the denial is even more problematic. The awkward wording seems to be governed more by a desire to protect human free will than to express doctrinal conviction in biblical categories. The two words that signal this are "require" and "cause." Left without qualification the reader must assume the natures of necessity and causality that the authors have in mind. But anyone who has tried to understand the Bible's use of these ideas knows that there are many pitfalls to be avoided.

For example, we could ask, "Who caused Jesus' death?" Various answers could be legitimately given. The soldiers who nailed Him to the cross did. Judas did. The Jewish leaders did. Pilate did. All of these play causal roles in the death of Jesus. But Scripture also plainly teaches that God did. "The Lord was pleased to crush him, putting him to grief" (Isaiah 53:10, NASB).

At Pentecost Peter brings the divine and human causalities together in his sermon to the Jews. "This Jesus, delivered up according to the definite plan and foreknowledge of God, you crucified and killed by the hands of lawless men" (Acts 2:23). He attributes the death of Jesus both to his hearers' lawlessness and to God's sovereignty. This understanding of divine and human causality permeated the spirituality of New Testament believers, as evidenced by their prayer after early experiences of persecution for their faith. After Peter and John were released from imprisonment they met with fellow believers and prayed together saying this, "Sovereign Lord, who made the heaven and the earth and the sea and everything in them,...truly in this city there were gathered together against your holy servant Jesus, whom you anointed, both Herod and Pontius Pilate, along with the Gentiles and the peoples of Israel, to do whatever your hand and your plan had predestined to take place" (Acts 4:24–28).

In recognition of this biblical perspective the Second London Confession of Faith (1689) wisely acknowledges that God uses secondary causes.

> Although in relation to the foreknowledge and decree of God, Who is the First Cause, all things come to pass immutably and infallibly; so that nothing happens to anyone by chance, or outside His providence, yet by His providence He orders events to occur according to the nature of second causes, either necessarily, freely, or contingently (chapter 5, paragraph 2).

Similar intricacies relate to the Bible's view of necessity. John 4:4 says that Jesus "had (*edei*) to pass through Samaria." It was necessary. Why? Because it was the shortest route? Jews regularly took the longer route because of the animosity between them and Samaritans. Because some force outside Himself coerced Him? Nothing in the text even hints at that. Rather, based on what happens next, this seems to have been a divine necessity for the fulfillment of God's saving purposes for many Samaritans.

The woman whom Jesus met at a well in Samaria had her life transformed by Him. She trusted Him. And as a result of her testimony so did many others (John 4:39). Did God's "sovereignty and knowledge require Him to cause" her "acceptance... of faith in Christ?" How can this question be answered with a simple "yes" or "no"? Yet, I think if you were to ask her if God caused her transformation she would have been unembarrassed to answer in the affirmative. That is certainly my testimony. I suspect it would be Paul's, as well. And if the question were put just that bluntly to them, I would hope that every Bible believing Christian would readily acknowledge that God is the one responsible for—or the one who caused—his or her salvation.

So while God uses all sorts of means in bringing about the salvation of sinners, He is the ultimate "cause" of that salvation. Other factors can certainly enter in (such as a faithful witness, a sermon, Bible study, prayer, kind deed, dramatic experience, etc.), but God is the one who effects it and thus, all glory belongs to Him.

Does God work in the same way to "cause" a person to reject Christ? Absolutely not. People are born rejecting Christ because they are by nature children of wrath (Ephesians 2:3). God is no less sovereign over those who reject Christ than those who trust Him savingly, but the only way a person stops rejecting Christ and begins to trust Him is through the sovereign, gracious work of God in his or her life.

11

Interacting with Article Eight

The Free Will of Man

ARTICLE EIGHT: THE FREE WILL OF MAN

We affirm that God, as an expression of His sovereignty, endows each person with actual free will (the ability to choose between two options), which must be exercised in accepting or rejecting God's gracious call to salvation by the Holy Spirit through the Gospel.

We deny that the decision of faith is an act of God rather than a response of the person. We deny that there is an "effectual call" for certain people that is different from a "general call" to any person who hears and understands the Gospel.

Genesis 1:26–28; Numbers 21:8–9; Deuteronomy 30:19; Joshua 24:15; 1 Samuel 8:1–22; 2 Samuel 24:13–14; Esther

3:12–14; Matthew 7:13–14; 11:20–24; Mark 10:17–22; Luke 9:23–24; 13:34; 15:17–20; Romans 10:9–10; Titus 2:12; Revelation 22:17

The affirmation could almost be acceptable due to its ambiguity were it not for the denial that removes all doubt of the authors' and signers' meaning. God does endow people with "the ability to choose between two options." Part of being human is to have volition. We are not puppets. We make choices every day. Who denies this?

When the affirmation refers to "actual" free will we are left to conclude that the concern is to affirm it in distinction to some other kind that is less than real. Any doubt about that conclusion is erased by David Allen, one of the most prominent signers and defenders of the document, in his article entitled, "Recovering the Gospel—Why Belief in an Unlimited Atonement Matters," which is a defense of Article Three.[15] Allen, the Dean of the School of Preaching at Southwestern Baptist Theological Seminary, reveals that compatibilism is the foil to the authors' and signers' "actual free will." Compatibilism basically teaches that God's meticulous sovereignty and predestination are compatible with and do not violate in any way the free moral agency of people. Speaking in behalf of the authors and signers, Allen writes, "[W]e deny compatibilism and affirm genuine freedom."

"Genuine freedom," Allen elaborates, exists only when an individual is able to choose between options. Where this is lacking, there is no actual freedom. This is what makes him reject the priority of regeneration to faith in salvation.

[15] http://sbctoday.com/recovering-the-gospel-why-belief-in-an-unlimited-atonement-matters-2/

> We do not believe that compatibilism comports with genuine freedom. The reason should be obvious. In this construct, God imposes regeneration, and the individual is "free" to exercise faith but he is not free to choose any differently. By any normal understanding of freedom, this is not freedom. In order to have freedom, there must be the opportunity for a genuine choice between at least two options, and there must be no coercion made with respect to the choice. Acts committed under compulsion are not truly free acts.

It seems that the kind of freedom that Allen and the other promoters of this document envision is contra-causal freedom, a belief that at any point in any situation, in order to have "actual freedom," one must be able to do otherwise. I am not competent to deal with all the philosophical assumptions that undergird such a view (to say nothing of the psychology and neurology involved). Fortunately, such competence is not necessary to understand how the Bible speaks of the human will and freedom.

In John 5:40 Jesus said to some Jews who were opposing him, "You are unwilling [*ou thelete*] to come to me so that you may have life." The problem was with their will. They would not choose to trust Him as Lord. That is the problem with every unbeliever. While it is true that the gospel enables us to say "whosoever will," it is also true that sin forces us to admit that the problem is that "whosoever" won't! At least, left to himself and his own power of choice he won't.

This is taught so plainly throughout Scripture that it should be hard to miss. I have already touched on this point in my review of Article Two, but it bears elaborating. Jesus said "No one *can* come to me unless the Father who sent me draws him" (John 6:44, emphasis added) and "No one *can* come to me unless it is granted him by the Father" (John 6:65, emphasis added). Paul writes, "For the mind that is set on the flesh is hostile to God, for it does not submit to God's law; indeed, it *cannot*. Those who are in the flesh *cannot* please God (Romans 8:7–8, emphasis added). "Can" in both English and New Testament Greek (*dunatai*) is a word of ability or power. Jesus and Paul both make universal absolute statements with Jesus stating the only remedy that can overcome sinful man's spiritual inability: the Father must "draw" the sinner or, as he puts it in verse 65, the Father must "grant" it to him.

This is precisely the same point Jesus made to Nicodemus in John 3. "Unless one is born again he *cannot* see the kingdom of God" (John 3:3, cf. v. 5). Sin has affected the human will and has done so in such a way that it is now enslaved to sin. Jesus said, "Everyone who commits sin is a slave to sin" (John 8:34).

Because the authors of this document do not regard the fallen human will to be enslaved to sin's power they cannot abide the teaching that regeneration gives rise to faith. Nor do they appreciate the fact that the grace that executes this new birth has caused many in evangelical history to describe it as "irresistible" or "effectual." In the words of David Allen, such teaching "vitiates free will." This judgment can only arise from a radically different understanding of Jesus' and Paul's teachings on sinful man's spiritual inability than what I gave above. By nature the sinner's will is enslaved to sin and what he needs is not encouragement but emancipation.

It is no violation of the will of a prisoner to open the prison door and remove his chains. It is no violation of the will of a dead man to bring him back to life. It is no violation of the will of a baby to have it conceived and brought into the human race. When Jesus stood before the tomb of Lazarus, after he prayed he loudly said, "Lazarus, come out" (John 11:43). Think about this scene. Jesus commanded Lazarus to do what he was unable to do. If Lazarus had the ability to come out of the tomb, he would not have needed Jesus to be there. But it was as the Word of the Lord was accompanied by the power of the Lord that the dead man was made alive. And when Lazarus was awakened, he responded and came out.

This is exactly what we do in evangelism. We call spiritually dead people to come to life. We call on those who do not have spiritual ability to repent and trust Christ. As we preach the gospel, we know that the Word of the Lord must be accompanied by the power of the Lord or no one will be saved. When God graciously does this saving work, it is not a vitiation of man's will. It is a gift of resurrection. Can you imagine Lazarus complaining that Jesus had vitiated his free will by granting him life?

Both statements in this article's denial are unfortunate. The first less so, because its awkwardness causes it to miss the mark at which I suspect it aims. The latter more so because it is imminently clear and states exactly what the authors intend to deny.

If by "decision of faith" the authors mean the act of trusting Christ, then of course it is not "an act of God." God does not believe for anyone. Sinners are those who must believe on the Lord Jesus in order to be saved. It is the individual's faith, not God's. In that sense, faith most certainly is "a response of the person." Again I ask, who in the SBC suggests otherwise? However, giving the authors the benefit of the doubt, I suspect they are primarily concerned to reject the idea that faith is a gift of God. In their scheme if this is true then faith cannot be a genuine response of the individual. Scripture, however, teaches that it is both (Ephesians 2:8–9; Philippians 1:29; Acts 16:31, etc.)

It can appear irrational to affirm that faith is both a gift of God and the duty of the sinner. That way of thinking is what gave rise to Joseph Hussey's "Modern Question" in eighteenth-century English evangelicalism. To see faith as a duty such that everyone should be under obligation to repent and believe seemed to Hussey and his followers to rob the Holy Spirit of His proper role in applying the gospel. Thus, they denied that faith is a duty. This article's denial seems to make the same mistake but instead of claiming that faith is not a duty it runs in the opposite direction and rejects the notion that faith is a gift of God. In his defense of this document Brad Reynolds sets forth an exegetical case that attempts to uphold this understanding.[16] He appears, however, to operate from the same "either/or" view that caused Hussey to deny that faith is a duty. Reynolds and the other supporters, however, conclude that faith is not a gift of God.

This seems to stem from a rationalistic approach to the nature of reality that does not fully appreciate the way God actually governs His world. This is where compatibilism comes in as a helpful tool that gives us a way to talk about reality as the Bible interprets it for us. For example, Joseph reflects this understanding of the world when he tells his brothers, in regard to their reprehensible and inexcusable abuse of him, "As for you, you meant evil against me, but God meant it for good" (Genesis 20:50). God sovereignly superintended the actions of his brothers, but not in a way that violated their freedom. They were responsible. They freely chose to sell Joseph into slavery but their free actions did not in any way make God contingent. As mentioned previously in my critique of Article Seven, the greatest paradigm for teaching us that God's absolute sovereignty is compatible with man's absolute responsibility is the death of Jesus (Acts 2:23).

[16] http://sbctoday.wpengine.com/a-commentary-onarticle-four-the-grace-of-godof-"a-statement-of-the-traditional-southern-baptist-understanding-of-god's-plan-of-salvation"/

The Apostle Paul even teaches this view principally in Philippians 2:12–13. "Therefore, my beloved, as you have always obeyed, so now, not only as in my presence but much more in my absence, work out your own salvation with fear and trembling, for it is God who works in you, both to will and to work for his good pleasure." We are responsible to work out *because* God works in us not only to do His good pleasure but to will to do it. This is simply the way that God has designed the world to work.

The final statement in Article Eight strikes me as the most clearly unbiblical one. "We deny that there is an 'effectual call' for certain people that is different from a 'general call' to any person who hears and understands the Gospel." Though it is true that the phrase "effectual call" is not found in the Bible, neither is the word, "Trinity." Both, however, are taught there. There can be no doubt that the Bible speaks of being "called" in ways that simply cannot be applied to people who hear the gospel yet never repent and believe.

Romans 8:28–30 is plain enough to make the case. "And we know that for those who love God, all things work together for good, for those who are called according to his purpose" (28). Is this a promise that belongs indiscriminately to believers as well as to unbelievers who have heard the gospel and yet remain in unbelief? If the authors of this statement are correct, then there is no other alternative. "For those whom he foreknew he also predestined to be conformed to the image of his Son, in order that he might be the firstborn among many brothers. And those whom he predestined he also called, and *those whom he called*, he also *justified*, and those whom he justified, *he also glorified* (29–30, emphasis added). If there is no distinction between the call of God that results in salvation through the effectual working of His Spirit and the general call of the gospel that goes out every time it is preached, then we are forced to conclude from this "golden chain of salvation" that everyone who is called by hearing the gospel will be justified and glorified.

The authors of this statement are far from universalists. But the argument that they have put forth in this denial leads to the error of universalism when we see the unbroken, efficient relationship between calling and glorification.

Historically, Southern Baptists have recognized the biblical teaching on effectual calling. The Philadelphia Baptist Confession of Faith dedicates a whole chapter to it. The opening paragraph of chapter 10 says this,

> Those whom God hath predestinated unto life, he is pleased in his appointed, and accepted time, effectually to call, by his Word and Spirit, out of that state of sin and death in which they are by nature, to grace and salvation by Jesus Christ; enlightening their minds spiritually and savingly to understand the things of God; taking away their heart of stone, and giving unto them a heart of flesh; renewing their wills, and by his almighty power determining them to that which is good, and effectually drawing them to Jesus Christ; yet so as they come most freely, being made willing by his grace (chapter 10, paragraph 1).

The Sandy Creek Baptist Association, which contributed so much to the establishment of the SBC, likewise affirmed effectual calling in Article IV of their Principles of Faith.

> IV. We believe in election from eternity, effectual calling by the Holy Spirit of God, and justification in his sight only by the imputation of Christ's righteousness. And we believe that they who are thus elected, effectually called, and justified, will persevere through grace to the end, that none of them be lost.

The late W. A. Criswell also held this historic Southern Baptist position. In a 1983 sermon on Romans 9:15–16 preached at First Baptist Church in Dallas, Texas, he made the following observations.

> *There is a general call, but there is also an effective call.* In the great general call, most of them did not respond, most of them did not hear, most of them did not believe, most of them did not come; but always some came, some heard, some were saved—*the effectual calling of God.*
>
> I read in Acts 13, verse 48, "When the Gentiles heard this, they were glad, and glorified the Word of the Lord: and as many as were ordained to eternal life believed." I turn the page again, and I read in 2 Thessalonians chapter 2, "Brethren beloved, because God hath from the beginning chosen you to salvation, whereunto He called you by our gospel." *There is an effectual call.* There are those who listen. God opens their hearts. God speaks to them, and they hear their name called, and they respond; *the effectual calling of the elective choosing Spirit of the Lord* (emphasis added).[17]

If the nineteenth-century churches of the Philadelphia Baptist Association, the Charleston Baptist Association or the Sandy Creek Baptist Association could not sign this statement, then can it honestly be called a statement on the "*Traditional* Southern Baptist Understanding of God's Plan of Salvation?" Furthermore, if W. A. Criswell's preaching diametrically contradicts this statement, shouldn't Southern Baptists be suspicious that its authors and supporters want to lay claim to representing traditional Southern Baptist thinking? Far more important than

[17] https://www.wacriswell.com/sermons/1983/the-effectual-calling-of-god1/

any historical claim, however, if the Word of God does not support this article, but actually teaches contrary to it, then neither Baptists nor any other evangelical Christians should be willing to approve it.

12

Interacting with Article Nine
The Security of the Believer

ARTICLE NINE: THE SECURITY OF THE BELIEVER

We affirm that when a person responds in faith to the Gospel, God promises to complete the process of salvation in the believer into eternity. This process begins with justification, whereby the sinner is immediately acquitted of all sin and granted peace with God; continues in sanctification, whereby the saved are progressively conformed to the image of Christ by the indwelling Holy Spirit; and concludes in glorification, whereby the saint enjoys life with Christ in heaven forever.

We deny that this Holy Spirit-sealed relationship can ever be broken. We deny even the possibility of apostasy.

John 10:28–29; 14:1–4; 16:12–14; Philippians 1:6; Romans

3:21–26; 8:29,30; 35–39; 12:1–3; 2 Corinthians 4:17; Ephesians 1:13–14; Philippians 3:12; Colossians 1:21–22; 1 John 2:19; 3:2; 5:13–15; 2 Timothy 1:12; Hebrews 13:5; James 1:12; Jude 24–25

As have all Particular Baptists throughout history (but not all General Baptists, with whom the authors of this document seem to identify most closely) this article affirms the permanence of salvation. Such a position is most certainly worthy of being designated the historic or "traditional" Southern Baptist view…not that it has been without detractors throughout SBC history.

The most notable, recent opponent to this view in the SBC was the late professor of theology at The Southern Baptist Theological Seminary, Dale Moody. In his 1981 *magnum opus*, *The Word of Truth*, Moody takes great delight that his is the first Southern Baptist theology textbook to reject all "five points" of Calvinism.[18] To Moody, this made perfect sense in light of the widespread rejection of the other four points. After the publication of his systematic theology Moody's consistent, five-point Arminianism came under increasing attack until he was finally relieved of his seminary teaching responsibilities in 1983 because of his affirmation of final apostasy.

This response to Moody is indicative of a consistent conviction held by Southern Baptists throughout their history. Southern Baptists have always firmly confessed that all who are true saints will persevere in faith. The Abstract of Principles of 1858 gives a complete article to this subject.

[18] Dale Moody, *The Word of Truth* (Grand Rapids, MI: Wm. B. Eerdmans, 1981), 337–365.

XIII. Perseverance of the Saints

> Those whom God hath accepted in the Beloved, and sanctified by His Spirit, will never totally nor finally fall away from the state of grace, but shall certainly persevere to the end; and though they may fall, through neglect and temptation, into sin, whereby they grieve the Spirit, impair their graces and comforts, bring reproach on the Church, and temporal judgments on themselves, yet they shall be renewed again unto repentance, and be kept by the power of God through faith unto salvation.

In language that borrows heavily from the Abstract, the Baptist Faith and Message 2000 also affirms this doctrine in plain language.

> All true believers endure to the end. Those whom God has accepted in Christ, and sanctified by His Spirit, will never fall away from the state of grace, but shall persevere to the end. Believers may fall into sin through neglect and temptation, whereby they grieve the Spirit, impair their graces and comforts, and bring reproach on the cause of Christ and temporal judgments on themselves; yet they shall be kept by the power of God through faith unto salvation (Article V, paragraph 2).

Both of these statements wisely acknowledge the reality of backsliding in a Christian's life. The stark, unqualified denial of "even the possibility of apostasy" by authors of this "traditional" statement unfortunately lacks that careful theological nuance. For although Dale Moody was wrong, the New Testament texts to which he appealed (most notably, Hebrews 6:4–8, 10:26–27; 2 Peter 2:20) cannot be ignored. There is such a thing as temporary apostasy (backsliding) and it should be distinguished from final apostasy when the issue of perseverance of the saints is addressed. This final apostasy is not the loss of once-held salvation but the evidence of false conversion (1 John 2:19). Sadly, some false converts never apostatize outwardly from confessing Christ as Lord in this life, only to find their unrepentant disobedience to God's commands betraying a false faith, a false conversion and an inward apostasy at the last judgment (Matthew 7:21–23). The authors need to be clearer when they say "we deny even the possibility of apostasy." Left unqualified, such a statement may embolden the unrepentant confessor to live in sin with a false assurance of salvation. John Owen provides great help at this point, in his *Nature of Apostasy*.[19]

This article's good affirmation of eternal security does raise one question that, if the authors and promoters would address, could further meaningful dialogue with those who reject their view of libertarian freedom. If the nature of fallen man's will is such that he has the power of contrary choice either to trust Christ or reject Christ, how and why is this power lost once such a man becomes a Christian? Why must a Christian always remain a Christian? How can God keep Him in the faith without "vitiating" his free will? It seems like this scheme leaves Christians with less of an "actual free will" (as Article Eight designates it) after conversion than before. These questions are sincere and I hope that the promoters and defenders of this document will address them.

The hermeneutic that rejects unconditional election and effectual calling of believers cannot sustain, with consistency, their eternal security. Patrick Hues Mell, one of the most prominent and influential founders and early leaders of the SBC (served

[19] http://www.monergism.com/thethreshold/sdg/owen_natureapostasy.html

17 years as president of the convention) understood this well and represented the standard original Southern Baptist view of the issue in his book, *Predestination and the Saints' Perseverance* (originally published as a series, ironically, in the *Georgia Christian Index*). Mell's biblical arguments show the inconsistency of trying to live in an Arminian house with a Calvinistic padlock on the door.

Though I think Article Nine could be strengthened by a brief statement that acknowledges the possibility of false conversions as well as real, temporary backsliding by believers, overall its affirmation and denial delineate the historic Baptist understanding of the permanent nature of eternal life. Our Lord Himself assures us that no one will be able to snatch His sheep out of His hand or the Father's hand (John 10:27–30) and the Apostle Paul confidently asserts that nothing can separate us (believers) from the love of Christ. "For," as he writes, "I am sure that neither death nor life, nor angels nor rulers, nor things present nor things to come, nor powers, nor height nor depth, nor anything else in all creation, will be able to separate us from the love of God in Christ Jesus our Lord" (Romans 8:38–39; cf. 8:35–37).

13

Interacting with Article Ten

The Great Commission

ARTICLE TEN: THE GREAT COMMISSION

We affirm that the Lord Jesus Christ commissioned His church to preach the good news of salvation to all people to the ends of the earth. We affirm that the proclamation of the Gospel is God's means of bringing any person to salvation.

We deny that salvation is possible outside of a faith response to the Gospel of Jesus Christ.

Psalm 51:13; Proverbs 11:30; Isaiah 52:7; Matthew 28:19–20; John 14:6; Acts 1:8; 4:12; 10:42–43; Romans 1:16, 10:13–15; 1 Corinthians 1:17–21; Ephesians 3:7–9; 6:19–20; Philippians 1:12–14; 1 Thessalonians 1:8; 1 Timothy 2:5; 2 Timothy 4:1–5

This is a wonderful article and a proper note on which to end a Baptist declaration of faith. Baptists have been and remain a "Great Commission people." William Carey, who is widely recognized as the Father of the Modern Missionary movement, was a Baptist. Through his faithfulness and the herculean efforts of his friends and fellow pastors, Andrew Fuller, John Ryland, Jr, John Sutcliffe and Samuel Pearce, the gospel was propagated beyond the shores of England into the borders of India in the late 19th century. It was their vision and devotion that gave rise to the "Particular Baptist Society for the Propagation of the Gospel Amongst the Heathen" in 1792.

Similarly, in 1812 Adoniram and Ann Judson were among the first Christian missionaries to travel overseas from America to India. Though Adoniram left his homeland a paedobaptist, after studying the issue of baptism in preparation for meeting the famous Mr. Carey, he arrived on those distant shores a convinced Baptist. Through his labors and those of Luther Rice, The Triennial Convention was established in 1814 for the purpose of supporting the work of Judson in Burma. This body was the precursor to the Southern Baptist Convention that marks its beginning in 1845. The SBC was organized to serve churches specifically by "eliciting, combining, and directing the energies of the denomination for the propagation of the gospel." The Great Commission is the DNA of the SBC.

Through the years Southern Baptists have been willing to contend earnestly to maintain and recover the purity of the gospel but they have never been content to be hoarders of it. It is precisely because "there is salvation in no one else, for there is no other name [than Jesus] under heaven given among men by which we must be saved" (Acts 4:12) that Southern Baptists have seen themselves as charged with a stewardship to take this gospel—the gospel of Jesus Christ and Him crucified—to the nations.

CONCLUSION

When I originally wrote this critique of the "Statement of the Traditional Southern Baptist Understanding of God's Plan of Salvation" I was unsure what its impact would be within the SBC. My desire was that it might serve to give some stable talking points over the doctrinal differences that exist between the more Calvinistic people in the convention and those who are less so. To a degree, that has happened. I have had the opportunity, personally, to discuss elements of this document both formally and informally with some of its most notable proponents.[20] Though I do not think those conversations have resulted in significant shifting of convictions, they have resulted in better understanding of our differences.

Biblical theology is important. The theology of salvation is of utmost importance. How we understand the Bible's teachings

[20] In March, 2015, I had the privilege of delivering the Darby/Beal lectures at the Baptist Missionary Association Theological Seminary in Jacksonville, Texas. The theme of those lectures was the TS. One session was given to a discussion of the document by a panel that included Dr. Malcolm Yarnell of Southwestern Seminary (a signer of the TS) and me. Recordings of those lectures and that discussion are available online at https://www.sermonaudio.com/search.asp?currsection=sermonstopic&keyword=Darby+Beal+2015

about the way God saves sinners will inevitably impact both our worship and our witness. I have no doubt that the men whom I know and respect who have produced, signed and promoted the TS have great desires to honor the Lord and His Word and to see His gospel faithfully proclaimed around the world so that all who hear may be saved. I share those desires and would not want to do anything to hinder or detract from our cooperative efforts to make Jesus Christ known. I firmly believe that we agree on the essence of the gospel and on the necessity and immeasurable importance of evangelism and missions. Though we may have disagreements—even strong disagreements—on how that gospel actually works to save sinners, may we never forget those things on which we do agree as we carry on our fraternal debates. May the Lord enable us to move forward in this twenty-first century with an uncompromising commitment to the gospel of Christ and an unquenchable passion to see the nations bow before Him as Lord.

AFTERWORD

BY TOM NETTLES

In conclusion, "Traditional" Southern Baptist soteriology as defined in this document has asserted central evangelical and historically Baptist affirmations that every Southern Baptist should approve. They believe that human sinfulness makes the sinner under a sentence of condemnation. They clearly believe that the gospel of the blood and righteousness of Christ is a sinner's only hope, outside of which there is no salvation. They believe that repentance and faith are the human responses through which one receives eternal life, and that the response of faith is not meritorious. They believe that all of the saved are secure and that God forestalls any of them from falling away. They believe the church should be engaged in mission to preach the gospel to the ends of the earth. So should we all affirm each of these truths; and if that is a sufficient basis of agreement then we should be free to teach, preach and otherwise propagate our respective understandings of the relation between divine sovereignty and human responsibility without the cloud of ouster darkening the horizon.

Given that, every reader of the document might notice some incongruities in the language that create an internal incoherence in the overall doctrinal structure as well as a misrepresentation of what the document ahistorically calls "New Calvinism." For example, how does the rejection of any "incapacitation of any person's free will" relate to the assertion that "no sinner is remotely capable of achieving salvation through his own effort" or that he "inherits a nature … inclined toward sin?" It would seem that the admission of a complete incapability and an inclination would doom the attempt to maintain the pure reality of "Free will." A marble placed on an incline will without fail, determinatively, move toward the lower part of the incline. Though the framers sought a word that did not seem so harsh as "bondage of the will" they chose a word that is a part of the vocabulary of determinism, for an incline determines the direction of a thing unless there is outside intervention. What does "incapacitation" mean? In a strict sense, Calvinists could agree with the bare assertion for they believe that humans, made in the image of God, still have in their created natures the capacity for "free will," that is, living eternally in a condition where the affections and understanding are so fixed on the good, right, and holy that nothing sinful can ever enter (Revelation 21:4, 27). So we agree that the Fall has not so dehumanized us that we have no *capacity* for "free will" but that by the Fall our soul has been so flooded with anti-God perversity that universally and unremittingly we are without righteousness, understanding, goodness, and we neither fear God nor seek Him, much less do we love Him with the singleness of heart required by the Law and by the logic of His intrinsic excellence (Romans 3:11–18). Their quest for a freedom that does not exist (Romans 6:17–19; 1 Corinthians 2:14), however, creates lack of symmetry and consistency and puzzling incongruities and ambiguities in other phrases throughout the document. "We deny that only a select few are capable of responding," so do we all, for absolutely none in their state of depravity are capable, having a present moral propensity against God (Romans 8:7, 8); "We deny that this atonement results in salvation without a person's free response," so do we all, for from the atonement flows the grace that secures the person's free response (Romans 8:32); "We deny that the decision of faith is an act of God rather than a response of the person," so do we all, for it is not God that is called on to believe, but the sinner who believes (Romans 4:3–5).

In spite of these difficulties, the purpose of the document is clear. Its signers desire to make a resolute stance against Calvinism and were willing to tolerate the nuances of ambiguity in order to be part of a flood-tide of remonstration against, as they perceive, a dangerous misinterpretation of the gospel. The document, therefore, denies eternal election of specific persons to salvation, accepts a substitutionary and propitiatory atonement but, in spite of its meritorious nature, suspends its effectuality on human decision rather than divine purpose, denies that grace is a purposeful and an effectual operation of God in both provision and bestowal of salvation and defines it as "God's generous decision to provide salvation" but all hangs on the will of a person inclined toward sin, denies the distinction between general call and effectual call, and makes the new creation, regeneration, the new birth, God's response to an unregenerate person's faith. In each case, many are the plans in the mind of God, but it is the purpose of Man that will stand (contra Proverbs 19:21).

The unproven assumption that whatever most Southern Baptists currently believe constitutes a defensible tradition is an uncertain way to do theology from generation to generation. One problem with this is that clarity of theological position among *most* Southern Baptists is not at all an easy thing to determine.

Out of the "vast majority of Southern Baptists" claimed by the "Traditionalist," some are Mormons, some are Jehovah's Witnesses, some migrate between Christian churches, Methodist churches, and Baptist churches, some play golf on Sunday or go boating or skiing with the family, some go to Wal-Mart instead of church and most of those would agree with the distinctive doctrines of this document. All of them likely assume free will, the universal undifferentiated love of God for all people (that is His job), and that grace is a general benevolence that we may respond to at any time we choose. A second difficulty is that this assumption relegates the sound orthodox years of 1845–1920 to a merely tolerable phase of Southern Baptist thought and treats it with a dismissive spirit. "For almost a century," the document says, "Southern Baptists have found that a sound, biblical soteriology can be taught, maintained, and defended without subscribing to Calvinism." Much of that hundred years was given to theological decline, particularly 1920–1980, and one should pause seriously before elevating those years of doctrinal broadening and apostasy and denominational heavy-handedness to a foundational position for today's Southern Baptist consensus. It is clearly demonstrable that Basil Manly, Sr. and Jr., Richard Fuller, R. B. C. Howell, P. H. Mell, J. P. Boyce, John A. Broadus, F. H. Kerfoot, J. B. Jeter, H. H. Tucker, B. H. Carroll, J.B., Gambrell and others would be ruled out of "traditional" Baptist theology of salvation by this document. Canonizing, by arbitrary fiat, a position that separates itself from a three and a half century confessional history, the early systematic theology textbooks written by Southern Baptists, and the preaching tradition of a noble company of pulpit expositors must surely strike the reader as eccentric and idiosyncratic. The hubris of an announcement that we have now consolidated a tradition dismissive of the pre-decline Baptist fathers is a staggering disappointment and unwarranted by the entirety of Baptist history.

The statement has been written, circulated, and presented as the advanced theological alternative for those that "do not want Calvinism to become the standard view in Southern Baptist life," apparently completing, with the exception of one point, the "clear trajectory ... away from Calvinism." If this is seen as an interpretation of the BF&M to rally the "vast majority" against a theology of the past, then its signers are wanting to reduce the room provided by clear doctrinal forms within the Baptist Faith and Message for Calvinists to function in good conscience. This phenomenon would surely turn Baptist History on its head. Gratefully, the constructor[s] has provided a large number of proof texts for the doctrinal affirmations and denials. These can be read carefully along with the statements they are intended to support. These constructions and proof texts can be compared with articles on the same subjects along with proof texts from a more seasoned Baptist confession of long and venerated tenure, the Charleston Association Confession. Perhaps this kind of comparison will provide a discussion that is theological, biblical, and historical and will serve us well in reaching a more stable condition of cooperation.

Appendix 1: A Statement of the Traditional Southern Baptist Understanding of God's Plan of Salvation

Authored by Eric Hankins

The following is a suggested statement of what Southern Baptists believe about the doctrine of salvation. Compiled by a number of pastors, professors, and leaders in response to the growing debate over Calvinism in Southern Baptist life, it begins with a rationale for such a statement at this time, followed by ten articles of affirmation and denial. The goal was to create a statement that would accurately reflect the beliefs of the majority of Southern Baptists, who are not Calvinists. The concern of the developers of this statement was that the viewpoint of this majority was not well-represented by the term "non-Calvinist" and that an instrument was needed by which that majority might articulate positively what they believe vis-à-vis Calvinism. There is no thought that this document reflects what all Southern Baptists believe or that it should be imposed upon all Southern Baptists. We believe that it does reflect what most Southern Baptists believe for good, biblical reasons. Its purpose is to engender a much needed Convention-wide discussion about the place of Calvinism in Southern Baptist life. If this Statement is reflective of your understanding of the doctrine of salvation in the life of the Convention, we would love for you to add your endorsement. To do so, see the instructions at the end of the statement and list of signers.

PREAMBLE

Every generation of Southern Baptists has the duty to articulate the truths of its faith with particular attention to the issues that are impacting contemporary mission and ministry. The precipitating issue for this statement is the rise of a movement called "New Calvinism" among Southern Baptists. This movement is committed to advancing in the churches an exclusively Calvinistic understanding of salvation, characterized by an aggressive insistence on the "Doctrines of Grace" ("TULIP"), and to the goal of making Calvinism the central Southern Baptist position on God's plan of salvation.

While Calvinists have been present in Southern Baptist life from its earliest days and have made very important contributions to our history and theology, the majority of Southern Baptists do not embrace Calvinism. Even the minority of Southern Baptists who have identified themselves as Calvinists generally modify its teachings in order to mitigate certain unacceptable conclusions (e.g., anti-missionism, hyper-Calvinism, double predestination, limited atonement, etc.). The very fact that there is a plurality of views on Calvinism designed to deal with these weaknesses (variously described as "3-point," "4-point," "moderate," etc.) would seem to call for circumspection and humility with respect to the system and to those who disagree with it. For the most part, Southern Baptists have been glad to relegate disagreements over Calvinism to secondary status along with other important but "non-essential" theological matters. The Southern Baptist majority has fellowshipped happily with its Calvinist brethren while kindly resisting Calvinism itself. And, to their credit, most Southern Baptist Calvinists have not demanded the adoption of their view as the standard. We would be fine if this consensus continued, but some New Calvinists seem to be pushing for a radical alteration of this long-standing arrangement.

We propose that what most Southern Baptists believe about salvation can rightly be called "Traditional" Southern Baptist soteriology, which should be understood in distinction to "Calvinist" soteriology. Traditional Southern Baptist soteriology is articulated in a general way in the Baptist Faith and Message, "Article IV." While some earlier Baptist confessions were shaped by Calvinism, the clear trajectory of the BF&M since 1925 is away from Calvinism. For almost a century, Southern Baptists have found that a sound, biblical soteriology can be taught, maintained, and defended without subscribing to Calvinism. Traditional Southern Baptist soteriology is grounded in the conviction that every person can and must be saved by a personal and free decision to respond to the Gospel by trusting in Christ Jesus alone as Savior and Lord. Without ascribing to Calvinism, Southern Baptists have reached around the world with the Gospel message of salvation by grace through faith in Christ alone. Baptists have been well-served by a straightforward soteriology rooted in the fact that Christ is willing and able to save any and every sinner.

New Calvinism presents us with a duty and an opportunity to more carefully express what is generally believed by Southern Baptists about salvation. It is no longer helpful to identify ourselves by how many points of convergence we have with Calvinism. While we are not insisting that every Southern Baptist affirm the soteriological statement below in order to have a place in the Southern Baptist family, we are asserting that the vast majority of Southern Baptists are not Calvinists and that they do not want Calvinism to become the standard view in Southern Baptist life. We believe it is time to move beyond Calvinism as a reference point for Baptist soteriology.

Below is what we believe to be the essence of a "Traditional Southern Baptist Understanding of God's Plan of Salvation." We believe that most Southern Baptists, regardless of how they have described their personal understanding of the doctrine of salvation, will find the following statement consistent with what the Bible teaches and what Southern Baptists have generally believed about the nature of salvation by grace through faith in Jesus Christ.

ARTICLES OF AFFIRMATION AND DENIAL

ARTICLE ONE: THE GOSPEL

We affirm that the Gospel is the good news that God has made a way of salvation through the life, death, and resurrection of the Lord Jesus Christ for any person. This is in keeping with God's desire for every person to be saved.

We deny that only a select few are capable of responding to the Gospel while the rest are predestined to an eternity in hell.

Genesis 3:15; Psalm 2:1–12; Ezekiel 18:23, 32; Luke 19.10; Luke 24:45–49; John 1:1–18, 3:16; Romans 1:1–6, 5:8; 8:34; 2 Corinthians 5:17–21; Galatians 4:4–7; Colossians 1:21–23; 1 Timothy 2:3–4; Hebrews 1:1–3; 4:14–16; 2 Peter 3:9

ARTICLE TWO: THE SINFULNESS OF MAN

We affirm that, because of the fall of Adam, every person inherits a nature and environment inclined toward sin and that every person who is capable of moral action will sin. Each person's sin alone brings the wrath of a holy God, broken fellowship with Him, ever-worsening selfishness and destructiveness, death, and condemnation to an eternity in hell.

We deny that Adam's sin resulted in the incapacitation of any person's free will or rendered any person guilty before he has personally sinned. While no sinner is remotely capable of achieving salvation through his own effort, we deny that any sinner is saved apart from a free response to the Holy Spirit's drawing through the Gospel.

Genesis 3:15–24; 6:5; Deuteronomy 1:39; Isaiah 6:5, 7:15–16;53:6; Jeremiah 17:5,9, 31:29–30; Ezekiel 18:19–20; Romans 1:18–32; 3:9–18, 5:12, 6:23; 7:9; Matthew 7:21–23; 1 Corinthians 1:18–25; 6:9–10;15:22; 2 Corinthians 5:10; Hebrews 9:27–28; Revelation 20:11–15

ARTICLE THREE: THE ATONEMENT OF CHRIST

We affirm that the penal substitution of Christ is the only available and effective sacrifice for the sins of every person.

We deny that this atonement results in salvation without a person's free response of repentance and faith. We deny that God imposes or withholds this atonement without respect to an act of the person's free will. We deny that Christ died only for the sins of those who will be saved.

Psalm 22:1–31; Isaiah 53:1–12; John 12:32, 14:6; Acts 10:39–43; Acts 16:30–32; Romans 3:21–26; 2 Corinthians 5:21; Galatians 3:10–14; Philippians 2:5–11; Colossians 1:13–20; 1 Timothy 2:5–6; Hebrews 9:12–15, 24–28; 10:1–18; 1 John 1:7; 2:2

ARTICLE FOUR: THE GRACE OF GOD

We affirm that grace is God's generous decision to provide salvation for any person by taking all of the initiative in providing atonement, in freely offering the Gospel in the power of the Holy Spirit, and in uniting the believer to Christ through the Holy Spirit by faith.

We deny that grace negates the necessity of a free response of faith or that it cannot be resisted. We deny that the response of faith is in any way a meritorious work that earns salvation.

Ezra 9:8; Proverbs 3:34; Zechariah 12:10; Matthew 19:16–30, 23:37; Luke 10:1–12; Acts 15:11; 20:24; Romans 3:24, 27–28; 5:6, 8, 15–21; Galatians 1:6; 2:21; 5; Ephesians 2:8–10; Philippians 3:2–9; Colossians 2:13–17; Hebrews 4:16; 9:28; 1 John 4:19

ARTICLE FIVE: THE REGENERATION OF THE SINNER

We affirm that any person who responds to the Gospel with repentance and faith is born again through the power of the Holy Spirit. He is a new creation in Christ and enters, at the moment he believes, into eternal life.

We deny that any person is regenerated prior to or apart from hearing and responding to the Gospel.

Luke 15:24; John 3:3; 7:37–39; 10:10; 16:7–14; Acts 2:37–39; Romans 6:4–11; 10:14; 1 Corinthians 15:22; 2 Corinthians 5:17; Galatians 2:20; 6:15; Colossians 2:13; 1 Peter 3:18

ARTICLE SIX: THE ELECTION TO SALVATION

We affirm that, in reference to salvation, election speaks of God's eternal, gracious, and certain plan in Christ to have a people who are His by repentance and faith.

We deny that election means that, from eternity, God predestined certain people for salvation and others for condemnation.

Genesis 1:26–28; 12:1–3; Exodus 19:6; Jeremiah 31:31–33; Matthew 24:31; 25:34; John 6:70; 15:16; Romans 8:29–30, 33;9:6–8; 11:7; 1 Corinthians 1:1–2; Ephesians 1:4–6; 2:11–22; 3:1–11; 4:4–13; 1 Timothy 2:3–4; 1 Peter 1:1–2; 1 Peter 2:9; 2 Peter 3:9; Revelation 7:9–10

ARTICLE SEVEN: THE SOVEREIGNTY OF GOD

We affirm God's eternal knowledge of and sovereignty over every person's salvation or condemnation.

We deny that God's sovereignty and knowledge require Him to cause a person's acceptance or rejection of faith in Christ.

Genesis 1:1; 6:5–8; 18:16–33; 22; 2 Samuel 24:13–14; 1 Chronicles 29:10–20; 2 Chronicles 7:14; Joel 2:32; Psalm 23; 51:4; 139:1–6; Proverbs 15:3; John 6:44; Romans 11:3; Titus 3:3–7; James 1:13–15; Hebrews 11:6, 12:28; 1 Peter 1:17

ARTICLE EIGHT: THE FREE WILL OF MAN

We affirm that God, as an expression of His sovereignty, endows each person with actual free will (the ability to choose between two options), which must be exercised in accepting or rejecting God's gracious call to salvation by the Holy Spirit through the Gospel.

We deny that the decision of faith is an act of God rather than a response of the person. We deny that there is an "effectual call" for certain people that is different from a "general call" to any person who hears and understands the Gospel.

Genesis 1:26–28; Numbers 21:8–9; Deuteronomy 30:19; Joshua 24:15; 1 Samuel 8:1–22; 2 Samuel 24:13–14; Esther 3:12–14; Matthew 7:13–14; 11:20–24; Mark 10:17–22; Luke 9:23–24; 13:34; 15:17–20; Romans 10:9–10; Titus 2:12; Revelation 22:17

ARTICLE NINE: THE SECURITY OF THE BELIEVER

We affirm that when a person responds in faith to the Gospel, God promises to complete the process of salvation in the believer into eternity. This process begins with justification, whereby the sinner is immediately acquitted of all sin and granted peace with God; continues in sanctification, whereby the saved are progressively conformed to the image of Christ by the indwelling Holy Spirit; and concludes in glorification, whereby the saint enjoys life with Christ in heaven forever.

We deny that this Holy Spirit-sealed relationship can ever be broken. We deny even the possibility of apostasy.

John 10:28–29; 14:1–4; 16:12–14; Philippians 1:6; Romans 3:21–26; 8:29,30; 35–39; 12:1–3; 2 Corinthians 4:17; Ephesians 1:13–14; Philippians 3:12; Colossians 1:21–22; 1 John

2:19; 3:2; 5:13–15; 2 Timothy 1:12; Hebrews 13:5; James 1:12; Jude 24–25

Article Ten: The Great Commission

We affirm that the Lord Jesus Christ commissioned His church to preach the good news of salvation to all people to the ends of the earth. We affirm that the proclamation of the Gospel is God's means of bringing any person to salvation.

We deny that salvation is possible outside of a faith response to the Gospel of Jesus Christ.

Psalm 51:13; Proverbs 11:30; Isaiah 52:7; Matthew 28:19–20; John 14:6; Acts 1:8; 4:12; 10:42–43; Romans 1:16, 10:13–15; 1 Corinthians 1:17–21; Ephesians 3:7–9; 6:19–20; Philippians 1:12–14; 1 Thessalonians 1:8; 1 Timothy 2:5; 2 Timothy 4:1–5

APPENDIX 2: POLEMIC THEOLOGY: HOW TO DEAL WITH THOSE WHO DIFFER FROM US

BY ROGER NICOLE

It seems strange that one should desire to speak at all about Polemic Theology since we are now in an age when folks are more interested in ecumenism and irenics than in polemics. Furthermore, Polemic Theology appears to have been often rather ineffective. Christians have not managed in many cases to win over their opponents. They have shown themselves to be ornery; they have bypassed some fairly important prescriptions of Scripture; and in the end, they have not convinced very many people—sometimes not even themselves! Under these circumstances one perhaps might desire to bypass a subject like this altogether.

We are called upon by the Lord to contend earnestly for the faith (Jude 3). That does not necessarily involve being contentious; but it involves avoiding compromise, standing forth for what we believe, standing forth for the truth of God—without welching at any particular moment. Thus we are bound to meet, at various points and on various levels, people with whom we disagree. We disagree in some areas of Christian doctrine. We disagree as to some details of church administration. We disagree as to the way in which certain tasks of the church should be pursued.

If we are careful to observe the principles that I would like to expound in this article, we may find that they are valuable not only in the religious field but also in the realms of politics, business and family. Who does not encounter from time to time people who are not in complete agreement? Whether it is between husbands and wives, parents and children, co-workers on the job or fellow members in the church, it is impossible to live without disagreement. Therefore it is good to seek to discover certain basic principles whereby we may relate to those who differ from us.

There are three major questions that we must ask; and I would like to emphasize very strongly that, in my judgment, we need to ask them precisely in the right order: (1) What do I *owe* the person who differs from me? (2) What can I *learn* from the person who differs from me? (3) How can I *cope* with the person who differs from me?

What Do I Owe to the Person Who Differs From Me?

Many people overlook the first two questions and jump right away to: "How can I cope with this? How can I bash this person right down into the ground in order to annihilate objections and differences?" Obviously, if we jump to the third question from the start, it is not likely that we will be successful in winning over dissenters. So I suggest, first of all, that we need to face squarely the matter of our duties. *We have obligations to people who differ from us.* This does not involve agreeing with them. We have an obligation to the truth, and that has priority over agreement with any particular person. If someone is not in the truth, we have no right to agree. We have no right even to minimize the importance of the difference. Consequently, we owe them neither consent nor indifference. But what we owe that person who differs from us, whoever that may be, is what we owe every human being—*we owe them love.* And we owe it to them to deal with them as we ourselves would like to be dealt with or treated. (Matthew 7:12)

How then do we desire to be treated? First, we want people to know what we are saying or meaning. If we are going to voice differences, therefore, we have an obligation to make a serious effort to understand the person with whom we differ. That person may have published books or articles. Then we should be acquainted with those writings. It is not appropriate for us to voice sharp differences if we have neglected to read what is available. The person with whom we differ should have evidence that we have read carefully what has been written and that we have attempted to understand its meaning. In the case of an oral exchange where we don't have any written words, we owe the person who differs from us the courtesy to listen carefully to what he or she says. Rather than preparing to pounce on that person the moment he or she stops talking, we should concentrate on apprehending precisely what his or her position is.

In this respect, Dr. Cornelius Van Til has given us a splendid example. As you may know, he expressed very strong objections to the theology of Karl Barth. This was so strong that Barth claimed that Van Til simply did not understand him. It has been my privilege to be at Dr. Van Til's office and to see with my own eyes the bulky tomes of Barth's *Kirchliche Dogmatik* (incidentally, these volumes were the original German text, not an English translation). As I leafed through them I did not see one page that was not constellated with underlining, double-underlining, marginal annotations, exclamation points, and question marks galore. So here is someone who certainly did not say, "I know Karl Barth well; I understand his stance; I don't need to read any more of this; I can move on with what I have." Each of the volumes, including the most recent, gave evidence of very, very careful scrutiny. So when we take issue with somebody, we need to do the job that is necessary to know that person so that we are not voicing our criticism in the absence of knowledge but that we are proceeding from the vantage point of real acquaintance.

Even that is not enough, however. Beyond what a person says or writes, *we must attempt to understand what a person means.* Now it is true that there are what are called "Freudian slips." That is, there are people who do not express themselves exactly in the way it should be done and in the process somehow they give an insight into a tendency that is in them all along and which leads them to express themselves in an infelicitous but revealing manner. So it is appropriate, I suppose, to note this as a personal footnote, so to speak, in order possibly to make use of it at some time in the discussion. But if somebody fails to express himself or herself accurately, there is no great point in pressing the very language that is used. We ought to try to understand what is the meaning that this language is intended to convey. In some cases, we may provide an opportunity for an opponent to speak more accurately.

I have experienced this in my own home. I have noticed that my wife sometimes says things like, "You never empty the wastebasket." Now as a matter of fact, on January 12, 1994, I did empty the wastebasket. Therefore, the word *never* is inappropriate! This tends to weaken the force of my wife's reproach. Well, I've learned that I don't get anywhere by pressing this point. This kind of response does not provide dividends of joy and peace in my home. I've learned, therefore, to interpret that when my wife says "never" she often means "rarely" or "not as often as should be." When she says "always," she means "frequently" or "more often than should be."

Instead of quibbling as to the words never and always, I would do well to pay attention to what she finds objectionable. And indeed, I should be emptying the wastebasket. Feminist or not feminist, a husband and father should empty the wastebasket; and therefore, if I fail to do this, even only once, there is a good reason to complain. Nothing is gained by quibbling about how often this happens. I ought to recognize this and be more diligent with it rather than to quote the dictionary.

Similarly, in dealing with those who differ, we ought not to split hairs about language just in order to pounce on our opponent because he or she has not used accurate wording. It is more effective to seek to apprehend what is meant and then to relate ourselves to the person's meaning. If we don't do that, of course, there is no encounter because this person speaks at one level and we are taking the language at another level. The two do not meet and the result is bound to be frustrating. If we really want to meet, we might as well try to figure out the meaning rather than to quibble on wording.

Moreover, I would suggest that we owe to people who differ from us to *seek to understand their aims*. What is it that they are looking for? What is it that makes them tick? What is it that they are recoiling against? What are the experiences, perhaps tragic experiences, that have steeled them into a particular stance? What are the things that they fear and the things that they yearn for? Is there not something that I fear as well or yearn for in the same way? Is there not a possibility here to find a point of contact at the very start rather than to move on with an entirely defensive or hostile mood?

As an example it may be observed that in the fourth century the heretic Arius, and undoubtedly many of his supporters, were especially leery of modalism, a serious error in the conception of the Trinity which claims that the Godhead manifested Himself in three successive forms or modes as Father, Son and the Holy Spirit rather than to exist eternally as Three Who have interpersonal relations with each other. From Arius' vantage point, the orthodox doctrine of the full deity of the Son and the Holy Spirit did of necessity imply a modalistic view. It did not help that one of his very vocal opponents, Marcellus of Ancyra, did, in fact, border dangerously on modalism. Arguments designed to show the biblical and logical strengths of the doctrine of the Son's full deity or vice versa the weakness of Arius's subordinationism would not be likely to be effective unless the instinctive fear of an implied modalism were addressed and shown to be without solid foundation. With all due respect to the soundness, courage, and perseverance of those like Athanasius and Hilary who consistently resisted Arianism, one may yet wonder if a more effective method of dealing with this error might not have been to allay the fear that orthodoxy inevitably would lead to modalism.

In the controversy between Calvinism and Arminianism, it must be understood that many Arminians (possibly almost all of them) believed that to affirm the complete sovereignty of God inevitably implies a rejection of any free will, power of decision, and even responsibility on the part of created rational beings, angelic or human. Their attachment to those features naturally leads them to oppose Calvinism as they understand it. It is imperative for the Calvinist controversialist to affirm and to prove that he does not, in fact, deny or reject these modalities of the actions and decisions of moral agents but that he or she undertakes to retain these—even though their logical relation to divine sovereignty remains shrouded in a mystery that transcends finite, human logic.

Similarly, the Calvinist should not glibly conclude that evangelical Arminians are abandoning the notion of divine sovereignty because they assert the freedom of the human will. It is plainly obvious that Arminians pray for the conversion of those yet unconverted and that they desire to recognize the Lordship of God. The Arminian will do well to emphasize this in discussion with Calvinists so as to provide a clearer perception of the actual stance of both parties. It is remarkable that committed Calvinists can sing without reservation many of the hymns of Charles and John Wesley, and vice versa that most Arminians do not feel they need to object to those of Isaac Watts, Augustus Toplady, or John Newton.

In summary, I would say we owe it to our opponents to deal with them in such a way that they may sense that we have a real interest in them as persons, that we are not simply trying to win an argument or show how smart we are, but that we are deeply interested in them—and are eager to learn from them as well as to help them.

One method that I have found helpful in making sure that I have dealt fairly with a position that I could not espouse was to assume that a person endorsing that view was present in my audience (or was reading what I had written). Then my aim is to represent the view faithfully and fully without mingling the criticism with factual statements. In fact, I try to represent them so faithfully and fully that an adherent to that position might comment, "This man certainly does understand our view!" It would be a special boon if one could say, "I never heard it stated better!" Thus I have earned the right to criticize. But before I proceed to do this, it is only proper that I should have demonstrated that I have a correct understanding of the position I desire to contest.

What Can I Learn from Those Who Differ From Me?

To raise the question, "What do I owe the person who differs from me?" is very important, for otherwise any discussion is doomed to remain unproductive. The truth that I believe I have grasped must be presented in a spirit of love and winsomeness. To do otherwise is to do detriment to truth itself, for it is more naturally allied to love than to hostility (Ephesians 4:15). Belligerence or sarcasm may, in fact, reflect a certain insecurity that is not warranted when one is really under the sway of truth. It may well be that God's servant may be moved to righteous indignation in the presence of those "who suppress the truth by their wickedness" (Romans 1:18). This explains the outbursts of the Old Testament prophets, of our Lord in His denunciation of the Pharisees, and of the apostles in dealing with various heresies and hypocrisies in the early church. These severe judgments were ordinarily aimed at warning members of the flock rather than winning over some people who had distanced themselves from the truth of God to a point which left no room for the hope of recovery (Psalm 139:19–22; Isaiah 5:8–25; Daniel 5:26–30; Matthew 12:30–32; Acts 7:51–53; Galatians 5:12; Revelation 22:15). But when dealing with those we have a desire to influence for the good, we need imperatively to remain outgoing and gracious.

When we are sure that our *outward* approach is proper, we need secondly to safeguard the *inward* benefits of courtesy. We need to ask the question, "What can I *learn* from those who differ from me?" It is not censurable selfishness to seek to gain maximum benefits from any situation that we encounter. It is truly a pity if we fail to take advantage of opportunities to learn and develop that almost any controversy affords us.

Could I be Wrong?

The first thing that I should be prepared to learn is that I may be wrong and the other person may be right. Obviously, this does not apply to certain basic truths of the faith like the Deity of Christ or salvation by grace. The whole structure of the Christian faith is at stake here, and it would be instability rather than broad-mindedness to allow these to be eroded by doubts. Yet, apart from issues where God Himself has spoken so that doubt and hesitancy are really not permissible, there are numerous areas where we are temperamentally inclined to be very assertive and in which we can quite possibly be in error. When we are unwilling to acknowledge our fallibility, we reveal that we are more interested in winning a discussion and safeguarding our reputation than in the discovery and triumph of truth. A person who corrects our misapprehensions is truly our helper rather than our adversary, and we should be grateful for this service rather than resentful of the correction. As far as our reputation is concerned, we should seek to be known for an unfailing attachment to the truth and not appear to pretend to a kind of infallibility that we are ready to criticize when Roman Catholics claim it for their popes!

Our reputation will be better served if we show ourselves ready to be corrected when in error, rather than if we keep obstinately to our viewpoint when the evidence shows it to be wrong. I should welcome correction. It renders a signal service to me! I should respond, "I was mistaken in this; I am glad that you straightened me out; thank you for your help." People who are unwilling to acknowledge their mistakes, by contrast, may be called stubborn and lose their credibility.

What are the Facts?

In the second place we may learn from one who differs that our presentation, while correct as far as it goes, fails to embody the truth in its entirety on the subject in view. Although what we assert is true, there are elements of truth that, in our own clumsy way, we have overlooked. For instance, we may be so concerned to assert the deity of Christ that we may appear to leave no room for His humanity. As a Calvinist, I may so stress the sovereignty of God that the reality of human decision may appear to be ruled out. Here again, I should feel grateful rather than resentful. The adversative situation may well force me to give better attention to the fullness of revelation and preclude an innate one-sidedness which results in a caricature that does disservice to truth no less than an actual error may do.

Many of the mainline elements of Christianity are thus, "two-railed," if I may express myself in a metaphor. Unity, yet threeness in God, immanence yet transcendence, sovereignty of God and yet reality of rational decision, body and soul, deity and humanity of the Mediator, justification and sanctification, divine inspiration of Scripture and human authorship, individual and corporate responsibility. One could multiply the examples. When one of the factors is overlooked, one is doing no better than the railroad operator who would attempt to run an ordinary train with only one rail (I do not speak here of monorails!). The person who differs from me may render me great service by compelling me to present the truth in its completeness and thus avoid pitfalls created by under-emphasis, over-emphasis and omissions. Thus my account will be "full-orbed" rather than "half-baked!"

What are the Dangers?

I may learn from those who differ from me that I have not sufficiently perceived certain dangers to which my view is exposed and against which I need to be especially on guard. I may find out notably that there are certain weighty objections to which I had not given sufficient attention heretofore. Here again, I must be grateful for a signal service rendered by the objector. Instead of being irked by the opposition, I should rise to the challenge of presenting my view with appropriate safeguards and in such a way as to anticipate objections that are likely to arise. For example, consider how the Westminster divines were led to express the doctrine of divine decrees (Confession 3, 1).

> God from all eternity did, by the most wise and Holy counsel of His own will, freely and unchangeably ordain whatsoever comes to pass; yet so as thereby neither is God the author of sin, nor is violence offered to the will of the creatures, nor is the liberty or contingency of second causes taken away, but rather established.

The three clauses following "yet so as thereby" are specifically designed to ward off misunderstanding and to meet objections commonly raised by Arminians or Arminianizing divines. The peculiar wisdom of setting up these safeguards in the first article of that chapter is the fruit of the bitter experiences made in more than half a century of controversy issuing in rich, balanced and nuanced expression of truth in the Westminster standards.

In France, certain barriers placed on bridges, terraces or quays are called "*garde-fous*", that is to say "safeguards for the crazy." They provide a fence to prevent those who are careless from falling off the edge. Those who disagree with us provide us with an opportunity to ascertain areas of danger in our view and to build "*garde-fous*" there. It would be a pity if we failed to take advantage of such an opportunity.

What about Ambiguities?

We may learn from those who object that we are not communicating as we should and that they have not rightly understood what we wanted to say. In this we can be benefited also, for the whole purpose of speaking (or writing) is to communicate. If we don't communicate, we might as well remain silent. And if we don't manage to communicate properly what we think, we have to learn to speak better. If ambiguities remain, and it is apparent from the way in which the other person reacts that ambiguities do remain, then we are challenged to make a presentation that is clearer, more complete, more wholesome, and one that will communicate better.

We have biblical precedent for this. The apostle Paul, for instance, anticipated objections which arise from misunderstanding of his doctrine. In Romans 6:1 he writes "What shall we say then? Shall we go on sinning so that grace may increase? By no means!" This objection provides a launching pad to articulate more fully his thoughts so that readers will not be permitted to wander away, but will gain a proper understanding of the truth. There are many other examples of this approach in the Pauline writings (Romans 3:3; 6:15, 19; 7:7, 13; Galatians 2:17, 19 etc.). Even our Lord took pains to rephrase or amplify some of His statements that the hearer had not rightly understood at first (Matthew 13:18–23, 37–43; John 11:12–14, etc.).

The effort made to clarify our thought for others will often result in clarifying it also for ourselves. We may thus secure a firmer hold upon the truth, a better grasp of its implications, and relationship to other truths, a more effective way to articulate and illustrate it. These are boons for which we may be grateful to those who differ from us.

When we give due attention to what we owe those who differ and what we can learn from them, we may be less inclined to proceed in a hostile manner. Our hand will not so readily contract into a boxing fist, but will be extended as an instrument of friendship and help; our feet will not be used to bludgeon another, but will bring us closer to those who stand afar; our tongue will not lash out in bitterness and sarcasm, but will speak words of wisdom, grace and healing (Proverbs 10:20, 21; 13:14; 15:1; 24:26; 25:11; James 3).

How Can I Cope with Those Who Differ from Me?

In the previous two sections, we sought to explore how to derive the maximum benefit from controversy both as to those who differ by being sure that we do not fail in our duty toward them, and as to ourselves in welcoming an opportunity to learn as well as an occasion to vindicate our position. Now after having given due attention to the questions, "What do I owe?" and "What can I learn?", it is certainly proper to raise the query, *"How can I cope with those who differ from me?"*

Now "coping" involves naturally two aspects known as "defensive" and "offensive." Unfortunately, these terms are borrowed from the military vocabulary and tend to reflect a pugnacious attitude which injects bitterness into controversies. We should make a conscious effort to resist that trend. Furthermore "offensive" is often understood as meaning "giving offense" or "repulsive" rather than simply "passing to the attack." It may therefore be better to use the adjectives "protective" and "constructive" to characterize these two approaches.

Biblical Arguments

In evangelical circles biblical arguments carry maximum weight if properly handled, for they invoke the authority of God Himself in support of a position. This is what Luther so eloquently asserted at the Diet of Worms, and what the Westminster Confession also bears witness to in these words:

> God alone is Lord of the conscience, and hath left it free from the doctrines and commandments of men which are in any way contrary to His Word, or beside it in matters of faith or worship (WCF 20, 2).

We need here to be careful to make a reverent use of Scripture, quoting every reference in a way that is consistent with its context. This will protect our approach against the legitimate criticisms levied against "prooftexting," a method that lifts scriptural statements from their environment, and marshals them as if they were isolated pronouncements vested with divine authority without regard to the way in which they are introduced in Holy Writ. A notable example of this wrong approach would be to claim that God sanctions the statement, "There is no God" because it is found in Psalm 14:1 and 53:1.

We must therefore be careful to use the Scripture in such a way that an examination of the context will strengthen, not weaken, the argument. Very few things are as damaging to a position as a claim to be grounded in the authority of God's Word, only to find that a more careful examination of the text in its context cancels out the support it was presumed to give. An argument of this type, like the house built on sand, "falls with a great crash" (Matthew 7:27).

Likewise, a well-advised person will be careful to avoid passages that "boomerang"—passages that are used as proof, but turn out to be more decisive against the view advanced. For example, some people quote Philippians 2:12, "Work out your own salvation with fear and trembling" and forget that Paul continues, "For it is God who works in you to will and to act ...."

All this demands that we should know the Word of God. God entrusted the sacred Scriptures to His people in order that they may search it diligently (John 5:39) and make it the object of their daily meditation (Psalm 119). To be acquainted with the whole counsel of God (Acts 20:27) must be the aim not only of "professionals" like pastors and professors, but of everyone who wants to be known as a Christian. To be sound in the interpretation, correlation and application of the Scriptures is the way "to be approved, a workman who does not need to be ashamed" (2 Timothy 2:15), and every child of God ought to aspire to that.

Protectively we may be aware of passages that are often quoted to invalidate a stance which we find scriptural. Sometimes we may anticipate this objection even before it is raised and be prepared to show how it does not undercut our view. If we have a particularly strong refutation, we may at times wait until the person who differs quotes the passage. In this way we may score the psychological advantage of destroying an argument thought valid. Even this however, must remain within the framework of "speaking the truth in love" (Ephesians 4:15).

In some cases it may be possible to show that the interpretation which would see in a particular passage an objection to the scriptural truth we are undertaking to advocate is simply improper and indefensible because it sets this Scripture in conflict with its context, or at least with the larger context of the unity of divine revelation. In other cases it may be sufficient to show that there are one or several plausible alternative explanations of this text that do not precipitate the alleged conflict. Since we are obliged to seek the unity of the truth, a plausible interpretation that averts a conflict may well deserve preference.

To sum up, we must ever strive to take account of the fullness of biblical revelation to have the boldness to advance as far as it leads, and the restraint to stop in our speculations where the Bible ceases to provide guidance. Polemic Theology in this respect is simply biblical light focused in such a way as to assist those who appear yet caught in some darkness.

General Arguments

These arguments direct their appeal to something other than the actual text of Scripture, namely to logic, history and tradition. While the authority involved is not on the same level as the Bible, the Word of God, it has a bearing on the discussions and must be considered by those who wish to make a strong case.

Appeal to Reason

Human reason, especially when not guided by divine revelation, is apt to go astray either in being unduly influenced by prejudice (what we call "rationalizing") or when reason forgets its proper limits and attempts to apply to the infinite what is valid only for finite categories. Nevertheless, reason is a divine gift to humankind, indispensable to the process of receiving, applying and communicating revelation (cf. J. I. Packer, *"Fundamentalism" and the Word of God*, pages 128–137). It is a part and parcel of God's image in humanity. To fly in the face of logic is to court self-destruction, for logic has a way to beat its own path in the process of history. Rational arguments may therefore be presented with propriety, and those advanced by people who differ from us must be addressed.

Constructively, it behooves me to show that my view is in keeping with the totality of revealed truth, with the structure of the Christian faith as an organism of truth. I will promote the acceptance of an individual tenet if I can show that it is inescapably related to some other element of the faith on which I and the one who differs from me have agreement. For instance, one who accepts the doctrine of the Trinity is pretty well bound to confess the deity of Christ and vice versa.

Specifically, it is in order to make plain the damaging or even disastrous effects that a departure from the position I advocate will logically entail. In doing this, I must carefully distinguish between the view that the other person actually espouses and the implication that I perceive as resulting from it. Failure to make this distinction has resulted in the ineffectiveness of much Polemic Theology. Christians have wasted a huge amount of ammunition in bombarding areas where their adversaries were not in fact located, but where it was thought they were logically bound to end up.

To struggle with a caricature is not a "big deal." And to knock down a straw man does not entitle one to the Distinguished Service Cross! To be sure, it is a part of the proper strategy to show those who differ that their view involves damaging implications that will be difficult to resist in the course of time, but one must remain aware that it is the present position rather than anticipated developments that must be dealt with.

Protectively, I need to face the objections that are raised against my view. Some of them are irrelevant because they are based on a misunderstanding of the issues. To deal with these will help me to clarify my position and to reassert it with proper safeguards against one-sidedness, exaggeration or misconceptions. For instance, I may show that definite atonement is not incompatible with a universal offer of salvation in Christ, even though the supporters of universal atonement frequently think it is. Other objections may be shown to be invalid because they apply to the view of those who differ as well as to mine. Still other objections may be recognized as peripheral, that is to say, difficulties that may or may not be resolved rather than considerations that invalidate a position otherwise established. For instance, some alleged contradictions between two passages of Scripture represent a difficulty for the doctrine of inerrancy rather than a discreditation of this otherwise well-established tenet of the faith. Obviously the most advantageous situation is found when an objection can be turned around to become a positive argument in favor of the view objected to. Jesus' treatment of the Old Testament Law in Matthew 5:21–42 is a case in point. It might appear to a superficial reader that in this text Jesus repudiates the authority of the Law, when in fact He confirms it and reinforces it by His spiritual interpretation.

Furthermore, it is sometimes effective to challenge a person who differs from us to articulate an alternative approach which we may then proceed to criticize. For instance, a person who denies the deity of Christ may well be pressed to give his or her answer to Jesus' question, "Who do you say that I am?" (Matthew 16:15). Any answer short of full deity may be shown as deeply unsatisfactory, as leading to some form of polytheism or as failing utterly to account for the facts of the life, death and resurrection of Christ. It may be hoped that those who have unsatisfactory views may then leave the smoldering ruins of their system and take refuge in the solid edifice of the faith "once for all entrusted to the saints" (Jude 3).

Appeal to History and Tradition

The course of history is a remarkable laboratory that permits us to observe the probable developments that issue from the holding of certain tenets. The decisions of councils or the pronouncements of confessions of faith are often geared to guard against erroneous opinions that God's people recognized as dangerous or even fatal to the faith. To neglect this avenue of knowledge is to risk repeating some mistakes of the past that an acquaintance with history might well have enabled us to avoid. The Christological debates of the fourth and fifth centuries should protect us from the twin errors of Arianism and Apollinarianism, of Nestorianism and Monophysitism without our passing through the convulsions that the church of those days experienced. The Reformation of the sixteenth century, similarly, should shield us from repeating some of the mistakes of the Roman Catholic Church.

Constructively, it is proper for me to attempt to prove that I am in line with orthodoxy in general and specifically with statements of faith that have received wide acceptance or that are part of the subordinate standards of my church or of the church of the one who differs. This will be especially significant if the formulation was established for the purpose of warding off a position analogous to that of my opponent. Now all man-made statements are subject to revision and correction, but it appears prima facie impossible that a view that flatly contradicts the Nicene Creed or even the Westminster Standards should turn out to be right, while these revered creeds, tested as they were through centuries of Christian thinking, should be wrong.

Specifically, the position of the one who differs may so closely approximate a well-known heresy adjudged as heterodox that the course of history may provide a portrayal of what happens to those who entertain it. The disastrous course of Arianism, culminating as it did in the Moslem conquest of North Africa, may be an example. We need, however, to be careful to recognize the importance of weighing all operative factors rather than just some selected ones which seem to suit our purpose. The demise of Christianity in North Africa applied largely to Egypt where a monophysite tendency prevailed, as well as to the lands that had been conquered by the Vandals with their Arian commitment.

Those who would gloat over the increasing heterodoxy of the Arminian movement in the Netherlands should probably be somewhat sobered in thinking of the destiny of Calvinism in New England, which moved from high orthodoxy around 1650 to the rather massive Unitarian and Pelagian defection at the beginning of the nineteenth century. These remarks do not invalidate the value of the lessons of history, but merely admonish to caution in applying them.

Protectively, the course of action would parallel closely what was described above. Objections raised against our view may be shown to be counterproductive, because they support rather than undermine our view. They also may be judged irrelevant, because they fail to address our real position or because they burden equally the objector's view. Or they may simply be inconsequential, because they have only a peripheral bearing on the issues.

Christian's Goal

Perhaps the most important consideration for the Christian is to remain aware at all times of the goal to be achieved. It is the consistent perception of this goal that will give a basic orientation to the whole discussion: Are we attempting to win an argument in order to manifest our own superior knowledge and debating ability? Or are we seeking to win another person whom we perceive as enmeshed in error or inadequacy by exposing him or her to the truth and light that God has given to us?

If the former be true, it is not surprising if our efforts are vain: we should be like physicians who take care of patients simply in order to accredit some pet theory. If the latter be true, we will naturally be winsome. This will increase our patience when the force of our arguments does not seem to have an immediate effect. This will challenge us anew to understand those who differ in order to present the arguments that are most likely to be persuasive to them. God has appointed all of us to be witnesses to the truth. (John 1:7; Acts 1:8) God is the one who can and will give efficacy to this witness. We should never underestimate His ability to deal even with those who appear most resistant. Who would have thought that Stephen could actually reach the heart and mind of anyone in the lynch mob that put him to death? But his great discourse was actually sowing goads in the very heart and conscience of Saul (Acts 26:14). Acts 7 shows that his argument was sealed by his Christ-like spirit in the face of this atrocious murder (Acts 7:59–60). His witness was used by God to win over perhaps the ablest of his adversaries, who was to be the great apostle Paul!

A Christian who carries on discussions with those who differ should not be subject to the psychology of the boxing ring where the contestants are bent upon demolishing one another. Rather "The Lord's servant must not quarrel: instead, he must be kind to everyone, able to teach, not resentful. Those who oppose him he must gently instruct, in hope that God will grant them repentance leading them to a knowledge of the truth, and that they will come to their senses…" (2 Timothy 2:24–26).